# The Báb
## The King of Messengers

*"O THOU Remnant Of God! I have sacrificed myself wholly for Thee; I have accepted curses for Thy sake, and have yearned for naught but martyrdom in the path of Thy love. Sufficient witness unto me is God, the Exalted, the Protector, the Ancient of Days."*

The Báb

A talk by Dr. Riaz Ghadimi
(published posthumously in English)

Translated by Riaz Masrour

JUXTA PUBLISHING LIMITED • HONG KONG

*To my wonderful and loving niece*

*Maryam Manteghi*

*a bright young lawyer and until recently a pioneer of Bosnia, who took in stride the harshest adversity life could throw her way and emerged unscathed and victorious and thus added to the love we hold for her feelings of pride and admiration for her unshakable courage, her joyful spirit and her unwavering faith.*

## Translator's Notes

Dr. Riaz Ghadimi, was a General of the Army, a doctor of medicine, an indefatigable teacher of the Bahá'í Faith and one of the most noted contemporary scholars and authors of the Faith of Bahá'u'lláh. He wrote on Islam and Christianity and produced a multitude of works on the Bahá'í Faith. His monumental multi-volume Arabic/Persian dictionary, *Riaz'u'l-Lughát (Heaven of Words)*, is a unique accomplishment of great value for future scholars and researchers in gaining a deeper understanding of the meaning and application of various words used in the Bahá'í scriptures.

On the night of 8 July 1984, Dr. Ghadimi delivered a two-hour lecture on the subject of "The Báb, the King of the Messengers" in Toronto, Canada. Hard copies of the presentation were later sold to those interested in the audience with all revenues going to the local Bahá'í Fund. In 1987 he revised and expanded the work into a small book. Some 6 years later, in 1993, he re-published the second revision of the work, which is the basis of the present translation.

## *Alláh'u'Abhá*

This treatise is not a book of history. It is the text of an address about the greatness of the revelation of the Báb. Part 1 covers highlights of the events and themes related to the life of the blessed Báb and also deals with the torment and suffering that afflicted that holy Being and the companions of that Manifestation of God. As well it describes the miserable and ignominious fate of the perpetrators of such deeds. Part 2 discusses the preeminence of the religion of the Bayán, the frequent and explicit references to the revelation of Bahá'u'lláh, the martyrdom of the Bayán's Author, as well as unnumbered believers of that precious revelation, and the loving sacrifice of the enormous power and influence of that supreme theophany in the path of the Blessed Beauty, Bahá'u'lláh.

## – Part 1 –

*At the break of dawn from sorrows I was saved*
>    *In the dark night of the Soul, drank the elixir I craved*
*Ecstatic, my soul was radiant, bright,*
>    *Sanctified cup of my life, drunk I behaved*
*O, what exalted sunrise, what glorious night,*
>    *That holy night, to the New Life I was enslaved*
*From now on in the mirror, O what a sight*
>    *The mirror, glory of my soul, proclaimed and raved.[1]*

Exactly one thousand years after the passing of Imam Hasan Askari, the last Imam of the blessed line of the Lord of the Age,[2] the appointed time anticipated by the followers of Islam, according to the prophecies of the Qur'an, reached its consummation when in AD 1844 the blessed Báb proclaimed His mission in Shiraz and transformed the "night" of the Islamic tradition by the dawning effulgence of His revelation heralding the promised emergence of the Sun of Singleness.[3]

The Báb was born on the first day of Muharram of 1235 AH (20th October of AD 1819) in Shiraz. The place of His birth was the upper floor of the home of the paternal uncle of His mother and His wife's father, Hájí Mírzá Siyyid 'Alí. His mother, Fátimih Bagum (Bagum is a title which signifies respect, e.g., lady), had recognized the sublime station of her glorious Son through the teaching efforts of the wife of Hájí 'Abdu'l-Majíd[4] and Hájí Siyyid Javád Karbalá'í.[5] She passed away in Karbala[6] in 1300 A.H. (October of 1883) in the year 40 of the Bábí calendar.

---

1   The verses are by the great Persian poet Hafez of Shiraz as translated by Sh. Shahriari.
2   Reference to Prophet Muhammad, peace be upon Him.
3   The expression refers to Bahá'u'lláh.
4   A believer of note.
5   Hájí Siyyid Javad Karbalaí came from a family of scholars. He attended the classes of Shaykhí luminaries Shaykh Ahmad Ahsaí and Siyyid Kázim Rashtí and subsequently spent some time in India where he perfected his studies in philosophy. Visiting Karbila, he met with the Letter of the Living, Mullá 'Alí Bastámí where he accepted the Faith of the Báb and eventually attained the presence of Bahá'u'lláh. He lived a life of service and fortitude and passed away in Kirman.
6   The holy city of Karbilá in Iraq is the site of the shrine of the martyred Imam Husayn, considered the most tragic event of Muslim history by the Shiites.

She has been honored by the Most Exalted Pen with the title of Khayr'un'Nisá."[7] His father, Muhammad Riḍá, had passed away in 1243 A.H. (1827) when the Báb was 8 or 9 years old, and thus He was placed under the supervision of His maternal uncle 'Alí, who was later to receive the title of the Most Great Uncle.

We are all well acquainted with the story of the Báb's early childhood and youth, and how He manifested evidences of keen intellect and supernatural wisdom at such a tender age. Hand of the Cause Hasan Balyuzi recounts that on the opening day of the class at Shaykh 'Ábid's "Maktab"[8] when only 5 years old, the Báb was assigned a seat between two twelve-year-old boys. One of these, Muhammad Ibrahím, who later became a well-known merchant, gives the following account of the events of that first day:

> On that day, the Báb sat respectfully looking intently at the written text of the lesson in front of Him, and yet unlike other students who read the lesson out loud in unison, as was the custom, He chose not to participate. When asked of the reason of His refusal to take part in the general recitation, He was heard whispering this verse from the great Háfíz:

> *Abuzz with Thy name is the kingdom of heaven*
> *What, I wonder has entrapped you in this earthly plane*

> At another time, in a class on religious doctrine some of the older students asked an abstruse question which puzzled Shaykh 'Ábid who promised to research the question with the Mujtahids[9] and provide the authoritative response at a later date. At that moment the Báb broke His silence and offering incontrovertible

---

7   The Best of Women.
8   A local and unregulated school for children where the Qur'an and Traditions were taught.
9   High ranking clerics with authority to interpret the canon law and issue definitive judgments.

proof and cogent argument resolved the issue,
which caused amazement and wonder among
all present. Shaykh 'Ábid asked where He had
gained such knowledge, and the Báb, reciting a
single verse from Háfíz answered:

*He who is touched by God's grace*
*Can do what Christ did, whatever the case*

It has also been written that at times the Báb
would arrive late for class or was absent
altogether. The concerned Shaykh 'Ábid would
send a few students to inquire about Him. They
would return and report that they found the
Báb in a prayerful state and thus did not disturb
Him. Once when He arrived late, Shaykh 'Ábid
asked of the reason that had kept Him. The Báb,
rather than remaining silent as was His
customary disposition, quietly responded that
He had been in the house of His Forefather and
that He wished He would be like Him!
Considering that the Báb was a Siyyid and a
descendent of the house of the Prophet
Muhammad, the significance of this statement
can readily be understood.


   Other such stories of various events associated with the life
of the Báb, as described by Shaykh 'Ábid and His classmates,
abound but are too lengthy for this summary presentation.
   The Báb attended the classes of Shaykh 'Ábid for a period of
six or seven years until He was 11 or 12 years old. At the age of
15, He became an associate in the commercial activities of His
uncle Siyyid 'Alí. He subsequently moved to Bushihr[10] and
resided there for some six years. Like the stories of His youth,
those regarding His extraordinary qualities of honesty and
integrity in His commercial dealings as well as His state of utter
devotion, attraction, and rapture as he performed His prayers

---

10  A city in southern Iran.

are just as astonishing and remarkable, and have been recorded
in the annals of the Faith of God.

In the *Dawn-breakers* Nabíl writes:

> The Báb was mostly engaged as a merchant in
> Bushihr and despite the city's intemperate
> climate and extreme heat He spent several
> hours a day on the roof top in a prayerful state.
> Although the sun's rays were intense yet His
> heart was so consumed by the love of His
> Beloved that He would hardly notice the heat
> and would continue with His prayers and
> supplications. Utterly forgetful of the world and
> all that was therein He would spend the hours
> between the early dawn and daybreak and from
> noon to early evening in a state of prayerful
> communion. At all times His attention was
> directed towards the city of Tihran as He
> welcomed and greeted the bright orb of the
> rising sun in a state of indescribable joy and
> rapture, a mystical allusion to the Sun of Reality
> whose rays were to illumine the entire planet.

> Yet the ignorant public suspected that He was
> worshipping the sun oblivious of the fact that
> His outward attention to the physical sun was a
> sign of His devotion to the Sun of Divine
> Reality that was yet to be made manifest. Siyyid
> Javád Karbala'í recounted that: Once when I
> was on a journey to India I arrived in Bushihr
> and since I had an established acquaintance
> with Mírzá Siyyid 'Alí I went to pay him a visit.
> I met the Báb at that time for the first time.
> Whenever we met signs of humility, kindliness
> and affection seemed to radiate from His face. I
> am utterly powerless to describe in words that
> luminous visage and that heavenly demeanor.
> All who knew Him, acknowledged the purity of

His being, the sweetness of His mannerism and conduct, His truthfulness and piety.

In the spring of 1841, the Báb made a journey to the Shiite holy shrines in Iraq lasting some seven months. In the city of Karbala, Siyyid Kázim Rashtí[11] frequently attained His presence. After His return to Shiraz, in August of 1842, the blessed Báb married Khadíjih Bagum, a cousin of His mother and two years His junior. In the following year He had a son who was named Ahmad and who passed away in childhood. The Báb regarded the boy as the first to be sacrificed in the path of His Beloved Lord and in a prayer expressed His boundless love in these words:

*O God, my God! Would that a thousand Ishmaels were given Me, this Abraham of Thine, that I might have offered them, each and all, as a loving sacrifice unto Thee. O My Beloved, My heart's Desire! The sacrifice of this Ahmad whom Thy servant 'Alí-Muhammad hath offered up on the altar of Thy love can never suffice to quench the flame of longing in His heart. Not until He immolates His own heart at Thy feet, not until His whole body falls a victim to the cruelest tyranny in Thy path, not until His breast is made a target for countless darts for Thy sake, will the tumult of His soul be stilled. O my God, my only Desire! Grant that the sacrifice of My son, My only son, may be acceptable unto Thee. Grant that it be a prelude to the sacrifice of My own, My entire self, in the path of Thy good pleasure. Endue with Thy grace My life-blood which I yearn to shed in Thy path. Cause it to water and nourish the seed of Thy Faith. Endow it with Thy celestial potency, that this infant seed of God may soon*

---

11  The famed Shaykhí teacher whose classes were attended by the Báb and who advocated the soon to be realized appearance of the Promised Qá'im.

*germinate in the hearts of men, that it may thrive*
*and prosper, that it may grow to become a mighty*
*tree, beneath the shadow of which all the peoples and*
*kindred of the earth may gather. Answer Thou My*
*prayer, O God, and fulfill My most cherished desire.*
*Thou art, verily, the Almighty, the All-Bountiful.*[12]

It must be noted that the "Afnán," or the branches of the
Divine Lote Tree, who are kinsmen of the Báb, are related to
Him mostly through the two brothers of His wife, Abú'l-Qásim
and Siyyid Hasan, and a number through His three maternal
uncles, namely, Siyyid 'Alí (the Most Great Uncle), Siyyid
Muhammad (the Great Uncle), and Siyyid Hasan-'Alí (the
Lesser Uncle).

On the eve of the 5th day of Jamadi'u'l-Avval of the year
1260 A.H. (23 May 1844), the Báb, then only 25 years of age,
proclaimed His mission to Mullá Husayn Bushrúyih, a
comprehensive description of which can be found in chapter 3
of *The Dawn-Breakers*. The first encounter between the Báb and
Mullá Husayn took place in an area outside of the town limits of
Shiraz known as "Goad Khazinih,"[13] where the Báb occasionally
visited for relaxation as well as for contemplation and
enjoyment of the surrounding's natural beauty. On that day,
accompanied by Mullá Husayn, the Báb returned home where
He made His declaration. Mullá Husayn is the first to believe in
the Báb. His other titles are: the First, the First Arrival, the First
to believe, the Bábu'l-Báb, the Báb and Siyyid 'Alí.

Prior to Mullá Husayn's confession of belief, the wife of the
Báb was aware that her Husband was endowed with an exalted
station. She recounts that from His actions, conduct and
disposition she had realized that He was a person of noble and
high rank but she never imagined He might be the Promised
Qá'im until the night of Mullá Husayn's visit. After dinner she
was given permission to retire to her bedroom but she could
hear the Báb's voice until dawn as He spoke with Mullá Husayn
or recited holy verses after which the historic event took place.

---

12 Nabíl Zarandí, *The Dawn-Breakers: Nabíl's Narrative of the Early Days of the*
*Bahá'í Revelation*, p. 77.
13 Literally the "Deep Pool".

The wife of the Báb, as attested by the Blessed Beauty, is the first woman to believe in Him. In 1299 AH (AD 1882) she passed away in Shiraz. In a tablet of visitation revealed by Bahá'u'lláh in her honor, He bestows upon her His blessings and adds that all the people who departed this life on the day of her passing received God's mercy and forgiveness:

> *I bear witness that on the night thou didst ascend to*
> *the Abhá Horizon and to the Sublime Companion*
> *and on the day that followed, God forgave the sins of*
> *every man or woman who had ascended, as a token*
> *of grace unto thee and as a bounty for thee, except*
> *those who had openly denied God and repudiated*
> *what God has revealed....*

Following Mullá Husayn, gradually the other Letters of the Living,[14] separately and of their own volition, recognized the station of the Báb and confessed their belief in Him. A list published in a number of historical accounts showing the names of the Letters of the Living and the order in which they came to recognize the Báb's station is inaccurate. The second individual to believe in the Báb, according to Nabíl, was in fact not Mullá Husayn's brother, as is generally held, but Mullá 'Alí Bastámí who accepted the new revelation some 40 days after the declaration of belief by Mullá Husayn. Mullá 'Alí Bastámí was the first of the Letters of the Living to set out, as instructed by the Báb, on a proclamation journey to Najaf in order to acquaint the greatest and the most renowned Shiite scholar, Shaykh Muhammad Hassan Isfahaní, the author of "Jawáhiru'l-Kalám,"[15] with the message of the Báb. He first visited Karbala and disseminated the glad tidings of the new revelation. He also met Táhirih in that city and recounted to her the events associated with the declaration of the Báb. He then traveled to Najaf and attended one of Shaykh Muhammad Hassan's classes and informed him of the news of the Báb's declaration and handed him His tablet in which he was addressed by name.

---

14  Letters of the Living are the first eighteen individuals who became believers in the Báb.

15  *The Spirit of Words – An exposition of sacred canons in Islam.*

This renowned Shiite scholar, then a resident of Najaf, had, over the course of 30 years of study and research, authored the well-known work, the "Jawáhiru'l-Kalám fi Sharh-i-Sharial'-Islam"[16] in several volumes. His fame had reached such heights that he became known as "the author of the Jawáhir" and "Chief of Scholars." He died in 1266 AH (1849).

Mullá 'Alí was judged to be an apostate and an atheist by this very same luminary and was delivered to the Ottoman authorities by his pupils and was subsequently transported to the Baghdad prison in chains. After months of imprisonment, he was dispatched to Istanbul, but after departing Mosul in a manner yet undiscovered, he was martyred. Mullá 'Alí is the first martyr of the Faith of the Báb. In 1262 AH (1846 CE), on Ottoman soil, he sacrificed his life for his Beloved.

Mírzá Muhammad 'Alí Bárfurúshí known to history as "Quddús", "the Last Point", "the Last to Believe" and "the Name of God, the Last", was a member of the Letters of the Living who, without requiring any proof or evidence, accepted the Faith at the very first moment he laid eyes upon the Báb. But Táhirih, even without the benefit of attaining His presence, declared her belief in a letter addressed to Him. She asked her brother-in-law Muhammad 'Alí Qazvíní, who at the time was departing from Karbala for Shiraz, to recite the following verse while delivering her letter into the hands of the Beloved of the world:

> The shining light of Thy face has dawned,
>> Why dost Thou withhold Thy call to sound?
> "Am I not Thy God?" Thy call would imply,
>> "Yea Thou art, Yea Thou art," will Thou hear our reply,

Of the eighteen Letters of the Living, six were from Khurasan (Mullá Husayn, his brother Mullá Muhammad Hasan, his nephew Mullá Muhammad-Báqir, Mullá 'Alí Bastámí, Mullá Khudábakhsh Qúchání and Mullá Hasan Bajistání), five were from Azerbaijan (Mullá Mahmúd Khu'í, Mullá Jalíl Úrumí, Mullá Ahmad Abdál Marághi'í, Mullá Báqir Tabrízí and Mullá Yúsuf Ardabílí. Mullá Báqir enjoyed a longer life than the other Letters of the Living and thus became known

---

16  Ibid.

as the "Letter of the Living"), three were from Qazvin (the
beloved Táhirih, Muhammad 'Alí, her brother-in-law, Hádí the
son of Mullá 'Abdu'l-Vahháb Qazvíní), two from Yazd (Siyyid
Husayn Yazdí and Mullá Muhammad Yazdí), one from
Mazindaran (Siyyid Muhammad 'Alí Bárfurúshí titled Quddús),
and one from India (Sa'íd Hindí).

Of these 18 individuals, 12 were martyred, nine of them in
the struggle at Tabarsi; they are: Mullá Husayn, Mullá
Muhammad Hasan, Mullá Muhammad Báqir, Mullá Yúsuf
Ardabílí, Mullá Jalíl Úrumí, Mullá Ahmad Abdál Marághi'í,
Mullá Mahmúd Khu'í, Mírzá Muhammad 'Alí Qazvíní and
Quddús. Mullá 'Alí Bastámí was martyred in Iraq, and two
others, Táhirih and Siyyid Husayn Yazdí, were martyred in
Tihran.

Having dispatched the Letters of the Living on various
teaching campaigns, in Sha'bán of 1260 AH (September of 1844),
the Báb, accompanied by Quddús and His Ethiopian servant, set
out for Mecca and the very heart of the world of Islam, the
Ka'ba, where He conveyed the announcement of His revelation,
in writing, to the Sherriff of Mecca[17] and verbally and openly to
Mírzá Muhít Kirmání, the most pompous Shaykhí scholar of the
time. He then set out for Medina but abandoned the idea of
proceeding to Karbala and in Safar of 1261 AH (1845) returned
to Bushihr.

Prior to His arrival He sent Quddús ahead to Shiraz to
deliver the Báb's "Khasá'il Sab'ih" or the "Seven Qualifications"
to Mullá Sádiq Muqaddas Khurásání[18] (who prior to accepting
the Faith of the Báb had earned the rank of Ijtihád or authority
to issue legal religious judgment) so that, when raising the call
of "Adhán" (Prayer) in the mosque, he may proclaim the news
of the new revelation to the people. He complied with the
directive, which led to his arrest as well as the arrest of Quddús

---

17  The highest ranking cleric of Mecca.
18  Mullá Sádiq Muqaddas Khurásání lived in Isfahan at the advent of the Báb
    and became a believer after the Letters of the Living. Along with Quddús,
    Mullá 'Alí Akbar Ardistání was among the first believers who were
    persecuted by the clergy and endured a thousand strikes of the lash. He
    received the title of "Asdaq" (the most righteous) or "Ism'u'lláh'ul'Asdaq"
    (the name of God- the most righteous) from the Báb and passed away in 1306
    A.H. in Hamadán. His life biography can be found in the work *Tazkirat'ul-
    Vafá*.

and Mullá 'Alí Ardistání.[19] Husayn Khán, Ajudán-Báshí, the governor of Fars, determined the penalties and ordered the punishment. Mullá Sádiq received many lashes; the beards of all three were burned, and they were subsequently dragged throughout the bazaars and streets amid the clamor and taunting of the populace. After subjecting them to much torment, they were expelled from the city.

The account of this event was printed in the *Times* of London as a news feature a few months later. This may well be the very first piece of news related to the new revelation published in the West.

---

19  An early believer.

**"THE TIMES"**         19 November 1845

# Mahometan Schism

A new sect has lately set itself up in Persia at the head of which is a merchant who has returned from pilgrimage to Mecca and proclaimed himself a successor to the Prophet. The way they treat such matters in Shiraz appears in the following account (June 23).

Four persons being heard repeating their professions of faith according to the form prescribed by the imposter were apprehended, tried and found guilty of unpardonable blasphemy. They were sentenced to lose their beard by fire being set to them. The sentence was put into execution with all the zeal and fanaticism becoming a true believer in Mahomet.

Not deeming the loss of beard sufficient punishment, they were sentenced the next day to have their faces blackened and exposed through the city. Each of them was led by a mirgazab (executioner) who had made a hole in his nose and passed through it a string which he sometimes pulled with much violence that the unfortunate fellow cried out alternately for mercy from the executioner and vengeance from heaven. It is the custom in Persia on such occasions for the executioner to collect money from the spectators and particularly from the shopkeepers in the bazaar.

In the evening when the pockets of the executioners were filled with money they led the unfortunate fellows to the city gate and turned them adrift. After which the mullahs at Shiraz sent men to Bushihr with power to seize the imposter and take him to Shiraz where on being tried he very wisely denied charge of apostasy laid against him and thus escaped from punishment.

Prior to this event, on his arrival in Shiraz from Bushihr, Quddús had been received by the Báb's uncle Siyyid 'Alí, and while in his company had delineated to him, to the extent that had come to pass, the details of the new Faith of God and disclosed the station of the Báb, which had led to Siyyid 'Alí's profession of belief. Five years later, in the episode of the "seven martyrs of Tihran,"[20] Siyyid 'Alí was the very first of the group to sacrifice his life in the path of the Báb.

---

20  The Seven Martyrs of Tihran is a famous and tragic event in the history of the new Faith. Four months prior to the martyrdom of the Báb, a number of the believers were arrested of whom seven of the most prominent and distinguished followers of the Báb were, at the command of the prime minister, Mírzá Taqí Khán (Amìr-Kabìr), martyred in the most incredibly savage fashion. They were:

1.  The Most Great Uncle of the Báb, Áqá Siyyid 'Alí – After his visit with the Báb in Chihríq prison, he returned to Tihran and while resident in the home of Mírzá Muhammad Bayk Chápárchi, was arrested by the authorities. The prime minister summoned him and ordered him to recant his Faith. Several of the prominent members of the merchant class mediated and proposed to pay a large sum for his release but Siyyid 'Alí would not budge from his position and drank the cup of martyrdom with astonishing courage. As he was brought to the place of sacrifice he was heard whispering the verse from the great Háfíz:

    *Praised be God for whatever I longed for*
    *He fulfilled better than what I had hoped for*

2.  Mírzá Qurbán 'Alí, one of the chief proponents of Mysticism was highly regarded by Mahd-i-Ulyá, mother of Násiru'd-Dín Sháh and many of the court notables. He was offered various high positions all of which only served to heighten his regard for the Báb and enflame his love for the Faith. On the day of his martyrdom while he embraced the bloodied and lifeless body of the Most Great Uncle he was heard murmuring the verse:

    *Happy the lover who in the path of his Beloved*
    *Wonders which to give up first, his head gear or his head*

    It took two strikes of the blade to silence him.

3.  Hájí Mullá Ismá'íl Farahání – was a highly regarded scholar and intellectual. A number of people offered to pay large sums for his life. When asked to recant his Faith, he cried out:

On His return from Bushihr to Shiraz, the Báb presented Himself to the officials of the governor of Fars province who had been dispatched for His arrest, and as recorded in detail in various historical accounts, He appeared before this governor of Fars, Husayn Khán Iraváni, and during the interview was insulted and struck in the face. Through the efforts of Imam Jum'ih and sponsorship of His uncle, He was released.

Following this event, the most influential individual to recognize the Báb was Siyyid Yahyá Dárábí, known to history as Vahíd, who was the son of Siyyid Ja'far Kashfí, a Muslim scholar of the highest rank. Vahíd, who was known to be able to recite some 30,000 Islamic Hadith[21] from memory, was entrusted by Muhammad Sháh the mission of investigating the Faith of the Báb. In three sessions he was so utterly overwhelmed and mesmerized by the Báb that he declared his belief.

In the summer of the third year of the Báb's declaration of His mission, on the 21st day of Ramadan of 1262 AH (23rd September of 1846), on the instructions of Husayn Khán, the

---

> *Tell Ismael, O, Sabá, from me*
> > *He who treads the path of sacrifice should see*
> *Returning alive from such a test*
> > *Is not a worthy choice of love's behest*

4.  Áqá Siyyid Husayn Turshízí – was a man of erudition and learning who had achieved to the lofty rank of Ijtihád in the field of religious jurisprudence. He had been converted through the efforts of Hájí Muhammad Taqí Kirmání. He, too, was instructed to recant his belief in the Báb. With astonishing audacity he refused and thus fulfilled the requirement of devotion and faithfulness to the Cause of his Beloved and attained to the desire of his heart.

5.  Hájji Muhammad Taqí – was a well-known and respected merchant of Kirmán who along with Áqá Siyyid Murtidá Zanjání and Áqá Muhammad Husayn Marághi'í were brought to the field of execution. Murtidá and Muhammad Husayn threw themselves on Muhammad Taqí and begged the executioner to be beheaded first. Thus three executioners beheaded them simultaneously.

     This event took place in Tihran some four months prior to the martyrdom of the Blessed Báb and two months after the struggle of Tabarsi (Rabi'u'tháni of 1266 A.H.).

21  Hadith or "tradition" is a hearsay account regarding the words and deeds of the Prophet Muhammad which are not corroborated in the Qur'an. There is thus no definitive evidence of their authenticity and various religious scholars have conflicting views regarding their legitimacy and therefore their applicability as part of authorized text.

governor, who himself had been ordered to murder the Báb, 'Abdu'l-Hamíd Khán, the chief of police, along with a number of government agents, attacked the house of the Báb. They climbed over the outer wall of the property, entered the house expecting to arrest a large number of Bábís but found and arrested only the Báb and His companion Siyyid Kázim Zanjání.[22] However, because of a sudden cholera epidemic in the city and the hasty departure of Husayn Khán from Shiraz, 'Abdu'l-Hamíd Khán whose own child had fallen ill with the dreaded disease, ordered the release of the Báb conditional on His leaving the city and pleaded with Him for the life of his child.

Having informed the governor of Isfahan of His intention to travel to that city, the following morning the Báb journeyed to Isfahan and spent some 6 months in that city (forty days in the house of Imam Jum'ih and four months in the Sun palace, the property of Manúchihr Khán, the Mù'tamidu'd-Dawlih the governor of Isfáhán). Manúchihr Khán's forefathers had been from Georgia[23] and were Christians. His father 'Abdu'l-Vahháb Isfahaní, was a well-known poet and wrote under the pen-name of "Nishát" (Joy). During the reign of Fath-'Alí Sháh, Manúchihr Khán had been the governor of Kirmanshah and Gilan, and from 1257 AH (1841) he had been entrusted with the administration of Isfahan, Luristan and Bakhtyari territories.

The stories related to his physical endurance, the strength of his hands, his prudence in management of affairs, and his zeal and courage are astonishing. His rank in the Faith of God is so lofty that 'Abdu'l-Bahá in a tablet of visitation revealed in his honor refers to him as "Siyyidu'l-Vuzará," (the Master Statesman), Maliku'l-Umará, (the King of Rulers), Shamsu'l-'Sudúr, (the Sun of Wisdom), Badru'l-Budúr, (the Full Moon of all Moons), Amír-i-Iqlímu'l-Athír, (the Ruler of the Ethereal Realm), Aljális 'Alá Saríru'l Majdu'l-Athíl (seated upon the throne of honor), Tha-shihámatu'l-Kubrá, (Possessed of the

---

22  Siyyid Kázim Zanjání was one of Báb's disciples who accompanied Him on His final journey from Shiraz to Isfahan and later out of Isfahan in September 1846. He was later martyred in Mazindaran. His brother was one of seven martyrs of Tihran.

23  Georgia became an independent country after the fall of communism in Russia

Most Great Courage), Sáhib-al-Turbatu'l-Ulyá, (the Possessor of
the Purest Dust), As-Sa'id fil-Mala'il-A'la, (the Happy One of
the Denizens of the Kingdom), Al-Majíd fí Malakutú'l-Abhá,
(the great one of Kingdom of Abhá), Al-Manut-bil-lisán Ahlu'l-
Taqwá, (Praised by the Tongue of the People of Piety), Al-
Mamdúh fí Alsun-i-Ashábu'l-Hudá, (Praised by the Tongues of
Those Who Are Guided).

At the end of his Tablet of Visitation, 'Abdu'l-Bahá writes:

> *Happy the one who visits thy luminous resting*
> *place, happy the one who kisses thy pure sepulcher,*
> *happy the one who holds close thine perfumed crypt,*
> *happy the one who breathes the fragrant earth of thy*
> *tomb, happy the one who would serve at thy musk-*
> *laden resting place, happy the one who would*
> *illuminate the site of thy burial chamber, happy the*
> *one who would adorn the novel site of thy grave, I*
> *swear by God that he is of those who have attained*
> *and will abide in the eternal paradise for evermore.*

The significant events of the Báb's sojourn in Isfahan and
the works revealed in that city, such as "the commentary of the
Súrih of "Val'Asr," which was revealed at the request of the
Imám Jum'ih; the work "the proof of the exclusivity of
prophethood," revealed at the request of Manúchihr Khán; as
well as the intense attraction of the people towards the Báb; the
report of these events to Mírzá Áqásí by the local clergy; the
issuance of their judgment for the murder of the Báb and other
events have been dealt with in detail in the first chapter of the
matchless work *God Passes By* and chapter ten of *The Dawn-
Breakers* and other books of history. And yet every event
associated with the life of that heavenly Being has given rise to
the manifestation of a dramatic and dazzling outcome.

One night the blessed Báb was a guest of Mírzá Ibráhím
Nahrí, the father of Sultán'ush-Shuhadá and Mahbub'ush-
Shuhadá,[24] who were no more than ten or twelve years old, at
his home in Isfahan. Mírzá Ibráhím who was the principal
deputy of the Sultánu'l-Ulamá (the town's chief cleric) confided
to Him that his brother Muhammad 'Alí and his wife had been

---

24  The King and Beloved of Martyrs respectively

unable to have a child. The Báb placed some food in a plate so that they may eat from it and remarked that according to the divine Will they will achieve the desire of their hearts. Subsequently, they became the parents of a daughter named Fátimih, who years later became the wife of 'Abdu'l-Bahá and was subsequently honored by Bahá'u'lláh with the title of Munírih.

Also in Isfahan at the instigation of Hájí Mírzá Áqásí there was an attempt for issuance of a fatwá (a religious judgment) to have the Báb murdered. However the prudent handling of the situation by Manúchihr Khán preserved the Báb who was, as seen by many witnesses, escorted out of the city of Isfahan and later surreptitiously brought back to the city and housed in the famed government house known as Qasr-i-Khurshíd (the sun palace).

Manúchihr Khán had many extraordinary and detailed plans for the triumph of the Cause. He wished to place his enormous wealth at the Báb's disposal and himself play the role of an intermediary between Him and the Sháh and on the Báb's behalf ask for the hand of one of Sháh's sisters in marriage. But the Manifestation of God did not consent to his worldly plan and disclosed to him his (Manúchihr Khán's) fast approaching death, which took place not long after. His nephew Gurgín Khán immediately alerted Mírzá Áqásí of the Báb's presence in Isfahan, which subsequently led to His arrest and exile.

Under guard, the Báb was moved to Kashan. In that town, on the Naw-Rúz of 1263 AH (AD 1847), the third new year since His declaration and the fourth year of the Badí' calendar, He sojourned for two days and three nights in the home of Hájí Mírzá Jání, who was later condemned to the dungeon of Tihran along with the Blessed Beauty and was subsequently martyred.

The Báb was then taken to Zanjan via the villages of Kinargird and Koulayn. In Zanjan, He stayed for a brief time in the caravansary of Mírzá 'Alí Muhammad Tabíb and was subsequently moved to Tabriz. (Tabíb became a believer in the Báb and Bahá'u'lláh, and some 20 years after the Báb's stay at his caravansary, in the presence of the governor and high-ranking clergy, he was beheaded in a tub and achieved the station of martyrdom in the path of God.

After a forty-day sojourn in Tabriz, the Báb was moved to
Máh-Kú. The Máh-Kú village and its prison were situated at the
summit of a mountain, which had but one entry or exit. The Báb
spent some nine months in that prison. At nights He was not
even allowed a lamp, and the cold was so intense that while
performing His ablutions for His prayers, the water would
freeze on His face.

Despite being Kurds and belonging to the Sunni branch of
Islam and thus avowed enemies of the Shiites, the governor and
the people of Máh-Kú nevertheless were so captivated and
enraptured by the Báb that in Jamádí of 1264 AH(April of 1848)
Hájí Mírzá Áqásí was forced to transfer the Báb from Máh-Kú to
Chihríq. In Máh-Kú due to 'Alí Khán Kurd's (the powerful ruler
of Máh-Kú) affection for the Báb, multitudes of believers
attained His presence. This included Mullá Husayn who
journeyed some 1,100 miles from Khurasan to attain His
presence in the Naw-Rúz of that year. Vahíd, too, was able, for a
second time, to gain admittance to that threshold. In that prison
the Persian and Arabic Bayán (the Mother Book of the Bábí
revelation) and the work "the seven proofs" along with nine
separate commentaries on the Qur'an and a great tablet
addressed to Muhammad Sháh and other tablets were revealed
and dispatched.

While imprisoned in Máh-Kú, other significant events also
occurred, including the incident in Qazvin whereby Mullá
Muhammad Taqí Baraqání was murdered by the hand of a
Shaykhí youth that resulted in the arrest and imprisonment of a
group of innocent Bábís and their subsequent dispatch to the
capital city. Another event was the first imprisonment of
Bahá'u'lláh in Tihran, which was carried out by order of Mírzá
Muhammad Shafí', the Justice Minister, for Bahá'u'lláh's having
given aid to the prisoners of Qazvin. Another major event was
the martyrdom in Tihran of Shaykh Sálih Karímí who counts as
the very first martyr of the Bábí cause in Iran. He had been one
of Táhirih's followers and had been converted to the Cause of
the Báb by her. At the time of his martyrdom, unfazed by the
circumstances, he recited this verse:

*To people I've left their religion and their world*
*Since I found you, O my Faith and my World*

Other major events were the martyrdoms of Hájí
Asadu'lláh, Mullá Táhir Shírází, and Mullá Ibráhím Mahallátí in
Qazvin; the arrest and imprisonment of Táhirih in Qazvin; and
her subsequent release due to Bahá'u'lláh's intervention.

To continue with the story, when Hájí Mírzá Áqásí
discovered the attraction of the people and governor of Máh-Kú
towards the Báb, he had Him transferred to the Chihríq Fort
near Salmás (Sháhpúr) on April 10, 1848 and placed Him in the
custody of Yahyá Khán the Kurd, who was the brother-in-law of
Muhammad Sháh and the uncle of Násiru'd-Dín Mírzá, the
crown prince. But before long Yahyá Khán became so enamored
by the Báb that he felt compelled to show the utmost
consideration and care during the entire period of His
imprisonment in Chihríq.

The Báb was imprisoned in Chihríq for a total of 27 months,
and yet, having captured the hearts and souls of the people, He
continued to counsel and guide them to the path of truth. The
attraction was such that the number of visitors who arrived to
visit the Báb exceeded the accommodating capacity of the
village. And although the inhabitants were of the Kurdish tribe
and belonged to the Sunni branch of Islam and were much more
fanatical than the people of Máh-Kú, yet the majority of them
were utterly captivated by the presence of the blessed Báb. In
that time a number of the believers attained His presence such
as Mírzá Assadulláh Khu'í, titled Dayyán, as well as the Báb's
Most Great Uncle who had been like a father to Him and who
subsequent to this last visit was arrested in Tihran and became
the first of the seven lovers who sacrificed their lives in the path
of the Báb in Tihran.

During the Báb's imprisonment in Chihríq the following
major events took place:

- After some three months, the Báb was moved from
  Chihríq to Tabriz on the direct order of Hájí Mírzá
  Áqásí, so that the 'ulamá could, under his orders, select
  whatever expedient they deemed fit to quench the fire
  of His Cause and His Person. Fearing a major

commotion in Khu'í, which was located along the
normal route of the journey, the Báb was taken to Tabriz
through the town of Urummiyih where in a show of
great excitement throngs of people enthusiastically
welcomed Him.

- The meeting for the examination and interrogation of
the Báb before the 'ulamá of Tabriz and in the presence
of Násiru'd-Dín Mírzá, the crown prince, was convened
in which the Báb openly declared His station as the
Qá'im, following which the 'ulamá voted for His
punishment. But the attendants refused to carry out the
penalty, and thus Mírzá 'Alí Asghar, the Shaykh'ul-
Islám, took the Báb to his own house and there
personally performed the punishment of bastinado on
His feet.

- Another event is the journey of Mullá Husayn to
Mashhad, which was followed by the arrival of Quddús
in that city and the turmoil created by their teaching
activities, the fame of Bayt-i-Bábyih (the Bábí house),
the arrest of Hassan, Mullá Husayn's man-servant, his
subsequent liberation by the hand of the Bábís and the
protest and cry of Yá Sáhib'uz-Zamán (O Possessor of
the Day of Judgment) by the Muslims in Mashhad, all of
which is recorded in detail in the latter part of chapter
14 and the beginning of chapter 16 of *The Dawn-Breakers*.

- And yet another major development was the
assemblage of the Bábís at the conference at Badasht
which was convened to announce the independence of
the religion of Bayán and the beginning of the new
world order. The conference took place in the summer
of 1848 and lasted 22 days during which Quddús,
Táhirih, and a group of some 80 believers were hosted
by Bahá'u'lláh. Details of this significant event are
recorded by the beloved Guardian in chapter 2 of his
*God Passes By*, as well as by Nabíl Zarandí in chapter 16
of *The Dawn-breakers*.

- Also there took place, on 4 September 1848, the death of
Muhammad Sháh, the flight of Hájí Mírzá Áqásí from
the court and his seeking asylum, the start of reign of

Násiru'd-Dín Mírzá, and the premiership of Mírzá Taqí Khán,[25] the Amír Kabír (the Great ruler).

The struggle at Tabarsi also counts as a defining point in the Bábí revelation. There, in accordance with the instructions of the Báb, Mullá Husayn with 202 of his companions, hoisting aloft the black standard, set out from Khurasan towards Mazandaran and on 12 October 1848 arrived at the outskirts of the shrine of Ahmad Tabaristání (Shaykh Tabarsi), who had been a prominent Islamic religious scholar and innovator. The shrine is located some 10 kilometers outside of the town of Barfurush (present day Babul). Taking a defensive stance, they occupied the shrine and constructed a number of walls and towers. Having inspected the fortifications on His visit to the Fort, Bahá'u'lláh caused the release of Quddús from his confinement in Babul and helped him to join the defenders of Tabarsi, where their number grew to some 313 souls. This number matched the number of Muhammad's companions in the battle of "Badr,"[26] which according to the hadith (tradition) should be the same number that would stand with the Qá'im when He arises.

These companions demonstrated extraordinary valor in defending themselves for seven months and frequently defeated the government forces that were dispatched against them and who were equipped with latest weaponry and heavy artillery. In one of the major defensive attacks undertaken by the companions, Mullá Husayn was martyred and the government forces were totally annihilated. Finally, Mihdí Qulí Mírzá, an uncle of the Sháh, affixed his seal on a copy of the holy Qur'an and took an oath that if the companions abandon the struggle no harm would come to any of them. But as they sat down to eat they were attacked and to a man, martyred. Quddús was taken to Babul and there according to the Fatwá of Sa'ídu'l-'Ulamá, was torn to pieces in the Sabzih-Miydán. Nabíl writes that they tortured him so savagely that the pen is powerless to depict.

---

25  Mírzá Taqí Khán was a man of great achievement and is considered, in Persian history, as one of the most astute statesmen to occupy the office of Prime Minister. He became the subject of the king's ire and was murdered, by his order, while taking a bath in Fin, Kashan.

26  One of Muhammad's battles with the idolaters

Bahá'u'lláh has commented that none who has born the torture of martyrdom has suffered as Quddús did, not even Jesus.

Another event was the martyrdom of the "Seven Martyrs of Tihran," which took place some four months prior to the martyrdom of the Báb. It ranks as one of the most astonishing epics of self-sacrifice and ready surrender of life in the path of the incomparable Beloved.

The conflict at Nayriz is yet another major event of this period. The great Vahíd and his companions perforce found refuge in the Fort of Khajou and there took defensive action and defeated all the invading forces until Zaynu'l-'Ábidin Khán, the governor of Niyríz and the commander of the forces, resorted to deception and fixing his seal on a copy of the Qur'an, took an oath not to harm any of the prisoners. And in this way he achieved his victory over the companions. Once victorious, he tortured and killed the entire group and their entire families in the most gruesome manner. Near the end of the conflict and some ten days before the martyrdom of the Báb, on 18 Sha'abán 1266 AH (29 June 1850) Vahíd himself was martyred.

The conflict at Zanjan ranks as one of the most significant events in Bábí history. Tens of thousands of army troops were defeated repeatedly at the hands of the three thousand companions of Hujjat[27] who had taken refuge in the Fort of 'Alí Mardán Khán. This conflict continued for some six months after the martyrdom of the Báb and eventually resulted in the martyrdom of Hujjat and some 1,800 of his companions.

After 27 months in the Chihríq prison and under instructions of Mírzá Taqí Khán, the Amír Kabír, the Báb was moved to Tabriz where the judgment for His execution had already been signed by the town's clerical establishment. He along with the immortal Anís (Mírzá Muhammad 'Alí Zunúzí) was brought to the field of martyrdom having been tied to a

---

27  Siyyid Muhammad 'Alí Zanjání, immortalized as Hujjat, accepted the new Faith early in the ministry of the Báb, after reading a few passages of His commentary of the Súrih of Joseph. He immediately set out to teach the new Faith to friend and stranger. The power of his logical and convincing argument and the courage of his presentation was astonishing. His defensive struggle at the Fort of 'Alí Mardán Khán in Zanján with some 3000 of his God intoxicated companions came to an end with his martyrdom.

wall before the guns of the regiment of Sam Khán, the Christian, and, as is recorded in various historical accounts, fired upon.

The bullets did not initially find their mark. After the Báb had completed His instructions to His amanuensis, the prisoners were again tied to the wall in such a way that Anís' head rested on the Báb's breast across from 750 troops of the Nasseri regiment under the voluntary command of Áqa Ján Bayk Khamsi'í. The lover and his Beloved became the target of 750 bullets. The martyrdom of the Báb took place on 28 Sha'aban of 1266 AH (9 July 1850). At the time the Báb was 30 years and six months of age, and some six years and forty-four days had passed from the date of His declaration.

The details of the martyrdom of the Báb, a reference to His exalted rank, and the description of the effects of this significant event can be found in chapter 4 of the Guardian's matchless work *God Passes By* and also in chapter 23 of Nabíl's immortal narrative.

The blessed Báb is known by some 40 different titles as have appeared in various Bahá'í Writings or have become customary terminologies among the believers some of which are:

*The Primal Point,*
*The Point around which circle the spirits of all Prophets*
*The Herald to the Most Great Abhá Luminary*
*The Point of the Bayán*
*The Unique Herald*
*The Morning of Truth*
*The Sea of Seas*
*The King of Messengers*
*The Most Great Prophet*
*The Most Great Remembrance of God*
*The Promised Qá'im*
*The Essence of Essences*
*The Most Exalted Father*
*The Father*
*The Spirit of Spirits*
*The Most Great Gate*
*The Mention of God, the Most High*
*The Unique mystery*

*The King of the Kingdoms of Bounty and Grace*
*The Morning of Truth*
*The Point*
*The Most Great Legislator*

Regarding Anís, Bahá'u'lláh has written:

> *We recall to mind at this point Muhammad before*
> *'Alí (Muhammad 'Alí) whose flesh became*
> *amalgamate with the flesh of his Lord, and his blood*
> *with His blood and his remains with His remains*
> *and his bones with the bones of his Almighty and*
> *Merciful Lord. My exalted pen testifies that he*
> *achieved to a rank never before achieved by anyone*
> *and befell him what no ear has heard its like. Upon*
> *him be My glory and the glory of My Kingdom and*
> *My habitation and the glory of the denizens of the*
> *cities of justice and fairness.*

## The Fate of the Oppressors

Those of high rank who held positions of responsibility and who rose against the Báb or His companions received terrible punishment and met with inauspicious ends in this world. Some of these are:

1.  The governor of Fars Husayn Khán Iravání, titled the Ájúdán Báshí or the Nizámu'd-Dawlih, imprisoned the Báb and ordered that He should be struck in the face. It was he, also, who ordered that Muqaddas receive a thousand lashes and that his beard and those of Quddús and Mullá 'Alí Akbar Ardistání be burned and that they be haltered and paraded through the streets and bazaars. After four years as governor, he was suddenly dismissed from office and was pursued by the government. He finally found refuge at the embassies of foreign governments and in 1858 died in hiding in utter ignominy and misery. In Bahá'í Writings he is referred to as: the vicious Husayn and the Tyrant of the Land of Shín (Shín refers to Shiraz).

2.  Gurgín Khán, nephew of Manúchihr Khán, who
    informed Mírzá Áqásí of the Báb's whereabouts and
    caused the arrest and exile of the Báb from Isfahan was
    struck by diphtheria, which led to his suffocation. His
    title is "the Hateful Gurgín."

3.  Muhammad Sháh who approved the many early
    martyrdoms and the exile of the Báb to the mountains of
    Adhirbaijan was afflicted, at the age of 40, with a
    multitude of diseases that led to his early death in 1848
    after enduring much pain and suffering.

4.  Mírzá Áqásí, prime minister of Muhammad Sháh, was
    uneducated and had been a scoundrel and a clown in
    Tabriz. His wit caused him great pain as once while
    traveling on foot following along the caravan that
    included the personal carriage of Nessá Bagum, the
    daughter of Fath-'Alí Sháh, in jest, he made a comment
    implying that if the lady was looking for a husband, he
    would be happy to oblige. He was bastinadoed severely
    until he could no longer walk. Later on in Tabriz
    because of his wit, sense of humor, and ready speech, he
    was assigned as a teacher to the children of the Kalántar
    (Chief of police) and subsequently became the teacher to
    Muhammad Mírzá, the crown prince. When
    Muhammad Mírzá became Muhammad Sháh, he
    dismissed the great Qá'im Maqám Faráhání[28] called by
    Bahá'u'lláh, the "the prince of the City of Wisdom and
    Letters," and offered the office of prime minister to
    Áqásí.

    Hájí Mírzá Áqásí was the cause of the Báb's exile to
    the fastnesses of Adhirbaijan and prevented a face-to-
    face meeting between Him and the Sháh that the Báb
    had requested. He devised multiple plans for the
    murder of the Báb. In one of His works, the "Khutbih

---

28  Mírzá Abul-Qásim the son of Mírzá 'Isá, were both ministers of high rank in
    the Qájár royal dynasty of Persia. Both were authors of note and both were
    known by the title of Qá'im Maqám. However, the son achieved a more
    exalted position than the father, attained the lofty rank of the prime minister
    and became well known for his scholarship. What honor is greater than to
    have been described by the Pen of Bahá'u'lláh as the "Master of the city of
    wisdom and letters".

Qahríyyih" (Wrathful Homily), the Báb declared him
accursed of God and foresaw an ominous fate for him.
Some months later he aroused the king's ire and in fear
fled the court finding refuge in the shrine of
'Abdu'l-'Azím.[29] All of his possessions, including his
1438 villages and other properties that comprised real
estate and gardens, were expropriated. He subsequently
fled to Karbala, and there he rapidly sank into misery,
became a pauper and a beggar, and died in utter
destitution and wretchedness. His titles are "the Unwise
Minister," "the Mean-Spirited Áqásí," and "the Wicked
Minister."

5.  Mírzá 'Alí Asghar, Shaykhu'l-Islám[30] of Tabriz was the
divine who with his own hands had bastinadoed the
Báb. He became paralyzed in both legs, and gradually
the paralysis permeated his entire body causing a foul
odor to emanate from him. Eventually, he died in such
utter misery that the event of his death became a
byword and a curse prevalent among the people of
Tabriz. The curse "By God! May you die like the
Shaykhu'l-Islám" expressed the depth of disgrace and
humiliation to which his memory had sunk. Subsequent
to this event no one was ever promoted to the rank of
Shaykhu'l-Islám, and this position eventually ceased to
exist altogether. In Bahá'í Writings the use of the title
"Wretched Shaykhu'l-Isám" applies specifically to this
man.

6.  Násiru'd-Dín Sháh was the sovereign whose direct
orders or affirmation of existing judgments account for
the majority of the martyrdoms in the Bayán and Abhá
periods, the details of which would produce an
astonishing tale of the martyrs of the Alá and Abhá
times. His order for the extermination of the Bábís in
Tabarsi reads: "Annihilation of this group from the face
of the earth and the expanse of the universe is the
obligation of every person and is considered a religious
duty which is essential to the well-being of the Religion

---

29  A religious shrine near Tihran that has a history of serving as a sanctuary for
victims of injustice
30  A title given to the ranking cleric of any town

and the nation...." On the margin, in his own hand, he adds his direct order to the commander of the army Mihdí Qulí Mírzá:

> This is true Mihdí Qulí Mírzá. On this issue you must make your best effort. This is not child's play; it concerns our very Faith and belief. You must cleanse the land from this foul and wicked people in such a way that no trace of them shall remain. Certainly do your very best and also help strengthen our Láríjání servant so that he may complete this task as well as other frontier assignments with success.   (Safar'ul'Muzaffar 1264 AH)

And yet his majesty Násiru'd-Dín Sháh, the Most Great King, the Pivot of Universe and the Star of the Assemblage, failed in his attempt to eradicate the Faith of God from the face of the earth and the expanse of the universe such that no trace may be left.

How ironic that as of today Bahá'ís reside in more than 117,000 towns and villages in 218 countries of the world. There are some 188 National Spiritual Assemblies on the planet and more than 19,000 Local Spiritual Assemblies. Its scriptures have been translated into 802 languages and have been published in over 600 scripts. There are some 741 Bahá'í schools worldwide and seven official Bahá'í radio stations that serve to bring the teachings of Bahá'u'lláh to the generality of humankind. There are more than 1,000 social, economic agricultural, and health-related development projects implemented around the world by the Bahá'ís to serve local populations.[31] Of the unique and exquisitely designed Bahá'í Houses of Worship in the five continents of the globe, the vast international, national, and local Bahá'í institutions and Bahá'í centers, the matchless Bahá'í shrines and gardens in the Holy Land

---

31  Statistics provided are provided as per the date of the original lecture was delivered.

as well as the favorable response the Bahá'í Faith has
received from over two thousand races, tribes, and
minority religions, I will make no further mention, as
such details would require an entire book all its own.

Násiru'd-Dín Sháh, in accordance with accounts
recorded in non-Bahá'í sources, on the night prior to the
festival of the 50th anniversary of his reign, or the night
before the day of his death, had a dream. He dreamt
that the angels of torture and death are descending
upon the earth carrying a casket of fire in order to place
him in it. He awakened with a scream. His confidants
recommended that he should not sleep alone. But once
asleep he dreamt again. This time Mírzá Taqí Khán, the
Amír Kabír, appeared to him with blood-shot eyes
telling him that on the very morrow the realm and the
nation will be rid of him for good. At the same time, his
preferred concubine, sleeping next to him, screamed
and awakened. She described to him her dream in
which all the ceilings of the palace had collapsed over
them. It seems that the king's lack of a comfortable
night's sleep and the nightmares he himself had
described were not limited to the last night of his life.
Bahá'u'lláh in one of His tablets refers to the gloomy
and melancholic last years of his life in these words:

> *The king, May God assist him, is so afflicted*
> *that none except God is aware of his condition.*
> *Verily comfort and sleep have abandoned him as*
> *decreed by God, the Ordainer, the Wise.*

In any case that night the Sháh did not return to bed
and at dawn ordered his carriage to be driven to the
house of the cruel and blood-thirsty Mujtahid of Tihran,
Mullá 'Alí Kaní,[32] and he himself traversed the distance
to his house on foot. He described his dreams for the
Mullá, but Mullá 'Alí's optimistic interpretation of his
dreams failed to relieve his agitation so he set out in his
carriage towards the shrine of 'Abdu'l-'Azím. There he
was murdered by a bullet from Mírzá Ridá Kirmání's

---

32  Country's leading cleric and responsible for the martyrdom of many Bábís.

pistol and was thus dispatched to his proper and eternal abode (1313 AH). In the Bahá'í Writings he has been referred to as "the Chief Tyrant," "the King of Tyrants," "the Cruel Násir," and "the Hateful King."

7.  Mírzá Taqí Khán Amír-Kabír was the son of Mashhadí Qurbán, a cook in the service of the household of the great Qá'im Maqám Faráhání. He received his education in the house of Qá'im Maqám. When he reached the age of maturity, he demonstrated a keen intellect and thus advanced quickly and was subsequently sent to Russia as a member of a diplomatic mission. He then became the commander of the Adhirbaijan army and later rose to the position of inspector-general and the guardian of Násiru'd-Dín Mírzá and eventually was promoted to the office of prime minister of Násiru'd-Dín Sháh.

    He instigated and was responsible for all the Bábí martyrdoms during his ministry. The martyrdom of the Báb was the result of his machination and was carried out under his orders despite his advisors' recommendation to the contrary. Some eighteen months after the martyrdom of the Báb, he himself became the subject of the wrath of his sovereign and was exiled to Kashan, where, in Rabí'ul-Avval of 1268 AH (1852), in the "Fin" bathhouse he was murdered by the agents of the king. As he relaxed in the pool, he was held in place by those agents in the presence of 'Alí Khán Hájib'ud'Dawlih (the court minister) while the veins in his right and left wrists were cut open. He was made to watch helplessly as blood poured out of him until he too was dispatched to his destined end. In the Writings he is referred to as the "Cruel Commander," "the Blood-Thirsty Amír," "the Blood-Thirsty Taqí," and "the Faithless Commander."

8.  Áqá Ján Bayk Khamsi'í was the commander of the Násiri regiment who volunteered to execute the Báb. Six years later he was killed in the artillery bombardment of Khurramshahr by the British naval forces.

9.  The soldiers of the Násiri Regiment considered their act of execution of the Báb to be a source of pride. In the

summer of that year, while resting under the shade of
the wall of a building, two hundred and fifty of them
who were busily engaged in debauchery became the
victims of an earthquake. The structure collapsed and
all of them were killed. In the following year the other
500 soldiers were part of a rebellion that failed. They
were all arrested and on the order of Mírzá Sádiq Khán
Núri were executed. Their bodies were subsequently
torn apart so savagely that many people openly
attributed such an end to the heinous act they had
committed. Such views were immediately repressed
and were considered as blasphemous, and any further
mention of them was proscribed by the clergy.

10. Mullá Sa'íd Dív-Kulla'í (Bárfurúshí) or Sa'ídu'l-'Ulamá
    who martyred Quddús with such unabashed savagery
    was afflicted with a strange disease whereby his thirst
    could not be quenched, and, despite wearing several
    layers of heavy and woolen cloths and constant burning
    of logs in a fireplace in his room, he found no relief from
    the cold and his body temperature continued to drop
    until he became utterly disabled. His end came in 1270
    AH. Over time, his palace became the collection site for
    trash and refuse. People used his name as part of a
    curse, i.e., "May God turn your house into a garbage
    dump like that of Sa'ídu'l-'Ulamá." He has been
    referred to as "the Most Cruel," "the Merciless and
    Prejudiced Mujtahid," and "the Shameless Savage."

11. Mahmúd Khán Kalántar, Tihran's Chief of Police, was
    responsible for the martyrdom of Táhirih and many
    other Bábís. He became the target of Násiru'd-Dín
    Sháh's wrath and was accordingly dragged through the
    city with bound feet, after which his still living body
    was quartered and each piece was suspended on the
    city's major gates. His title in the Writings is "Mahmúd
    the Enemy."

12. Hájibu'd-Dawlih, Mírzá 'Alí Khán was responsible for
    the murder of unnumbered Bábís, including Siyyid
    Husayn Yazdí titled "'Azíz" who was the Báb's
    amanuensis. He was taken prisoner by one of the "Lur"
    tribe; his beard was pulled out, and he was forced to eat

it after which they put a halter on him and mounted him as a beast of burden. They subsequently violated his wife and children before his eyes. This individual should not be confused with Ja'far Qulí Khán Hájibu'd-Dawlih, who was responsible for the martyrdom of Varqá and his son Rúh'u'lláh and who later became insane and died of disease.

13. The people of Iran who in every hamlet and city collaborated with the 'ulamá and government officials and, according to Nabíl Zarandí, in astonishing casualness and even approval observed the historically unprecedented pogroms and tortures, soon experienced divine chastisement. An epidemic of plague and cholera as well as several horrific earthquakes and famine caused the deaths of thousands. Cholera alone, as attested by the Báb in the "Seven Proofs," in four years killed some 100,000 people, and yet they did not recognize the true cause of their calamity. The horrific earthquake that shook Shiraz in 1268 AH caused the death of 12,000 people. Terrible and severe famines, one after another, resulted in the tormented deaths of thousands of people who still remained unaware as to the real cause of all the pestilence. The friends implored the Blessed Beauty for forgiveness and mitigation of the calamity. Reference to these horrific events have been made in a number of Tablets of Bahá'u'lláh and 'Abdu'l-Bahá, and some letters of the Guardian. In one such Tablet Bahá'u'lláh reveals:

> *That ye had written regarding the famine in Iran. This was divine chastisement mentioned in various Tablets. In the year of the revelation of the Exalted Tablet (Tablet of the King) that was delivered by the hand of Badi', reference to hardships, calamities and famines in that country was explicitly revealed and thus divine chastisement surrounded the entire population. The gist of the revealed verse is this: if it were not due to considerations of the friends all would have perished....*[33]

33  Ishráq Khávarí, *Má'idih-i-Ásimání* (*Heavenly Sustenance*), pp. 36-37.

This was a summary of the highlights of the history of the life of the blessed Báb and the fate of those who rebelled against the Manifestation of God.

## – Part 2 –

This presentation concerns three subject matters:

- First is delineation and presentation of evidence and proof regarding the supremacy of the station of the Bábí Revelation as compared to all the former Dispensations that have appeared in various periods in history. As Bahá'u'lláh clearly states, "His rank excelleth that of all the prophets and whose revelation transcendeth the comprehension and understanding of all their chosen ones."[34]

- Second is showing that the most significant and momentous aim of the Bábí dispensation was to prepare the people to expect and welcome the Faith of Bahá'u'lláh and to declare their belief in the Abhá religion. Contrary to former times in which the glad-tidings of the future revelation were vaguely intimated, the Báb had explicitly and clearly referred to the event to follow, specifying name and date of appearance. How ironic that the people of darkness and the ignoble group who have raised Azal's unworthy standard chose to overlook His clear and repeatedly emphatic warnings and have clung to the word "Mustagháth"[35] ascribing to it interpretations contrary to the obviously intended counsels of the Bayán and creating what has been no more than the buzzing murmur of a fly. However, as the shameful clamor has since been silenced we will not consider it further. Here, it will suffice to quote a few of the relevant glad-tidings.

- Third is explaining the astonishing and incredible impact of the divine scriptures that flowed from this heavenly revelation and highlighting the fact that the beloved Báb sacrificed not only His own Being but also

---

34  Quoted from Bahá'u'lláh, *Kitáb-i-Íqán* (Egypt), p. 189.

35  The word Mustagháth, meaning "he who is invoked for assistance" which appears in the Bayán, has a numerical value of 2001 in the Abjad numerology. Those who rejected Bahá'u'lláh argued that the coming of "Him who God shall make manifest" will take place in such a year. It was a puny argument the effect of which lasted for only a brief time, a misty fog which was dissipated under the brilliant sun of Bahá'u'lláh's revelation.

the entirety of His religion—His foremost disciples and His greatest champions as well as the very effect and influence that His scriptures had instilled in the hearts of the people of the world—in the path of Bahá'u'lláh.

• • •

In order to explain the first subject, that is, the superior nature of the religion of the Báb, we must compare His Writings that are the fruits of His innate knowledge with those of former dispensations. Any such study clearly indicates that Báb's revealed scriptures which constitute the very core of His religion and are divinely inspired and originate in the influences of the Holy Spirit, are clearly beyond comparison with those of today's three established religions both in scope and substance. The comparison is more apt since the scriptures of these Faiths, unlike the religious systems practiced in the Far East, have not been subject to variation, alteration or textual corruption.

In order to do this, we first have to take a cursory look at the scriptures associated with the Authors of the three major religions of antiquity.

In the Mosaic religion, the only trace and the sole written document linked to the Author of that Faith is the Torah, which contains 5 sections, namely:

- Genesis, which contains stories of the creation of the universe and of man;
- Exodus, which describes the departure of the Israelites from Egypt;
- Leviticus, which contains religious instructions and divine commandments as well as penal laws and rules of animal slaughter. Also included is the explanation of the station of the progeny of Leviticus who himself was the third son of Jacob, a line to which Moses also belongs;

- Numbers, which fixes the number of individual Israelites in the second year of Exodus from Egypt. Other issues are also discussed here;
- Deuteronomy, which is a repetitious presentation of a number of the commandments.

*Torah* is a Hebrew word meaning religion or training. Not only is this book not written by Moses, but in fact the recording of its various parts and its final compilation took place some 1,000 years after His time by Ezra (the Writer) with the aid of a group of the learned and devoted faithful. Of course, the Commandments of Torah had been recorded by the early believers prior to and possibly in accordance with God's Will and were being kept in the "Ark of the Covenant," which had very likely been obliterated in the repeated destruction and burning of Jerusalem, the story of which is quite extensive. In studying the Torah you will note that it is replete with narratives and sagas and interspersed throughout the books of Exodus, Leviticus, and Deuteronomy one can also glean a few of the divine commandments.

In the third volume of His "Makátíb" 'Abdu'l-Bahá states:

> *The main Torah comprises the Tablets that were revealed to Moses and includes the commandments. The rest which consists of stories and legends were added later and are not authentic.*

The intent here is to show that in the Jewish religion no work has survived from the pen of the Author of that religion and what does exist are some of the commandments revealed for the Jewish people as appropriate to the elementary state of civilization prevalent at that time. Moreover, these commandments may be gleaned from amidst hundreds of strange stories and amazing legends describing the attack of frogs, flies, mosquitoes, and locusts; the death of the first-born child of both man and beast; the changing of water into blood; the parting of the sea; delivery of the supply of water and bread in the mornings and meat at nights other than Saturdays; and hundreds of similar tales, which if not personally read can hardly be imagined.

The remainder of the Old Testament comprises 34 books or treatises or articles from the Jewish prophets. The Old Testament prophets were 48 in number, the first of whom was Joshua and the last was Malachi. They are generally referred to as "Muh Nabí" which means 48 prophets (M = 40 and H = 8; vowels have no numerical value). Four of these were Major Prophets: Jeremiah, Isaiah, Ezekiel, and Daniel. It has been written that some of these treatises were not actually authored by any of these prophets and that they were instead written by devoted believers and produced in their memories or in their names, and therefore the works are simply associated with them.

For instance, some believe that the Book of Joshua was possibly written by someone other than Joshua several centuries after the event but that it contains the words of Joshua. Some relate the Book of Judges to Ezra and some to Nehemiah and others to Jeremiah. Some relate the production of the Book of Glad Tidings to Jeremiah and others to Ezra and also the compilation of the Book of Nehemiah is related to Ezra. The two Books on Kings are linked to Jeremiah and Ezra, and the compilation of the two Books of Esther and Job are linked to two unknown individuals written in consolation of the Jews for their suffering so many hardships and calamities in their bondage in the land of Babel. Even some do not associate the entire 150 Songs of David to Him but some to Solomon and others to Asaf the chief musician of Solomon. Sumerians believe solely in the first seven Books, namely, the five main Books and the Books of Joshua and Judges.

■ ■ ■

Evangel, which means glad-tidings, is also not penned by Jesus and was written by four of the initial believers, about His life in Hebraic and subsequently in Greek. These putative authors are Matthew and John who were disciples and Luke and Mark who belong to the early group of believers. Therefore, we have four Evangels, which have been recorded and arranged sometime in the second half of the first Christian century, the details of which remain unclear.

These four accounts contain the stories related to the life of Jesus and His teachings, counsels and commandments as remembered by these four believers. The oldest copies of the New Testament are works of compilation belonging to the 4th or 5th centuries of the Christian era, such as the Sinaitic copy of the St. Petersburg Museum, the Efraimieh copy that is kept in the National Museum of Paris, the Vatican copy in the Vatican, and the Alexandria copy of London. The Evangel recorded by Luke is the most comprehensive and that of Mark is the shortest. The three works written by Matthew, Luke, and Mark are very similar and contain the account of the life and sayings of Jesus. These are also called the "Synoptic Gospels." John's version is somewhat different from others and contains philosophic issues regarding the meaning of "the Word," "Holy Spirit," and the divinity of Jesus.

The balance of the New Testament consists of 23 treatises or books from Luke and John, and a number of other early believers and disciples:

- Book of Acts from Luke
- Fourteen letters from Paul
- One letter from Jacob
- Two letters from Peter
- Three letters from John
- One letter from Judas
- One Book of Revelations of John

And thus in Christianity as in Judaism no work was issued from the pen of Jesus Himself and thus what we see in the scriptures are stories about the life of Jesus as well as His teachings and counsels as written by the early believers.

■　■　■

The Qur'an was not penned by Muhammad. The revelation of verses, whether commandments or stories, took place as prompted by circumstances and was instantly memorized by a number of the believers or was written on tree leaves, stone tablets, animal skin, flat pieces of wood, or large bones. Some 45 individuals have been identified as the recorders of revealed scripture. The most famous memorizers of the Qur'an are 'Alí, Zayd-ibn-i-Thábit, 'Uthmán-ibn-i-Áffán, "Abdu'lláh Mas'úd, Abú Músá Ash'árí, Abú-Darda', and Abi-ibn-i-Ka'b. However, there were other scribes and memorizers, a number of whom later lost their faith and abandoned the religion, i.e., 'Abdu'lláh, brother of 'Uthmán.

The memorized versions of the Qur'an did not always agree with the transcribed versions, and therefore Abú Bakr, the first Caliph, instructed Zayd-ibn-i-Thábit to solicit the aid of a number of knowledgeable believers of the Quraysh tribe and the memorizers of the Qur'an and embark upon collection, compilation, and eventual generation of a formalized version of the Book. Having accomplished the task, Abú Bakr placed the completed version of the Qur'an in the care of Hafsih, daughter of Omar and the wife of the Prophet of God.

Years later, during the Caliphate of Uthmán-ibn-'Affán, the third Caliph, a wave of complaints and critical remarks from rank and file believers began to be received, indicating their deep concern that each tribe and each family group was reading a Qur'an that was different in content from other Qur'ans. Thus Uthmán ordered that four copies of the corrected version of the Qur'an compiled by Zayd be prepared in the Quraysh style of writing and dispatched to the major Islamic centers, and he decreed that all other versions be destroyed. (Some Shiites believe that 'Alí also destroyed his own version although there were significant differences between his copy and the final Uthman version, in order to prevent the possibility of dissension.)

The Holy Qur'an, so compiled and current among Muslims today, has 114 Súrihs and some 6200 verses. The largest Súrih is the Súrih of "Baqarih" or "Cow" and the smallest is the Súrih of "Kawthar" the name of a fountain or a river in Paradise, which contains only three verses.

The Qur'an was revealed over the course of some 23 years to Muhammad, 13 years in Mecca and 10 years in Medina. (Some verses were revealed outside of these two cities at the sites of His battles with unbelievers). Some 82 of the Súrihs are revealed in Mecca and 20 in Medina, yet there are major disputes regarding the origin of each Súrih.

And so the Qur'an is also not from the pen of the Prophet Muhammad, and the last collection of its verses, as well as their phraseology and the order in which they appear in the Book, happened some 15 years after the passing of the Prophet of God. This included the compilation of the verses into Súrihs and giving each Súrih a designation to simplify identification. This was at a time when the Arabs had neither the punctuation marks such as the "period" nor the proper transliteration methodology and the use of applicable vowels in order to fix the proper pronunciation of words, the absence of which could dramatically change their meaning.[36]

At that time 'Alí was aware of the significance of the vowels of the Qur'an, since in the Arabic language changing vowels not only can change a male noun to a female noun but also can alter the meaning of phrases and sentences altogether. However, the Arabs considered the addition of vowels to the Qur'an objectionable, and only later in the history of Islam was this view gradually moderated. It was not until the time of Hajjáj-ibn-i-Yúsif that periods and vowels were incorporated.

The mention of the above facts does not imply nor should it be considered as suggesting any skepticism or misgivings on the part of the people of Bahá in their regard for the authenticity of these sacred works. It is, however, an explanation of the method of the compilation of their contents and the manner in which they are linked to the divinely ordained Authors themselves. Armed with this knowledge, we are now able to draw an accurate comparison between these Works and the scripture of the Bábí Faith.

■ ■ ■

The revealed Works of the Báb, which in terms of quantity are several times the combined works of all the prophets who have gone before Him, have all been issued from His own pen or dictated to scribes in His presence and later reviewed and sealed. The magnitude of these Verses and Works are such that

---

36  In Arabic the word "Mahram" which means confidant and "Mujrim" which means criminal look precisely alike on paper with the difference being the addition of a single period and changing in pronunciation of two vowels.

the Guardian in his *God Passes By* writes, "The revelation of the
Báb, in terms of the sheer size of His Works and the vastness
and eloquence of their significances as revealed from His pen is
unmatched in the annals of religion."

In the *Kitáb-i-Íqán*, comparing the works of the Báb with all
existing sacred works, Bahá'u'lláh writes:

> The prophets 'endowed with constancy' whose
> loftiness and glory shine as the sun, were each
> honored with a Book which all have seen, and
> the verses of which have been duly ascertained.
> Whereas the verses which have rained from this
> Cloud of divine mercy have been so abundant
> that none has yet been able to estimate their
> number. A score of volumes are now available.
> How many have been plundered and have
> fallen into the hand of the enemy, the fate of
> which none knoweth.[37]

The Báb Himself while being interrogated in the presence
of the heir to the throne stated that within a space of two days
and two nights he revealed verses equivalent to the entirety of
the Qur'an , and in yet another passage He bears witness that
until His imprisonment in Máh-Kú the bulk of His revealed
works exceeded some 500,000 verses (Half a million verses in
three years compared to six thousand verses of the Qur'an in 23
years).

The names of some of the Báb's works are:

1. *Commentary on the Súrih of Joseph,* which according to
   Bahá'u'lláh is the Báb's "first, mightiest and greatest
   book."[38] The Súrih of Joseph as revealed in the Qur'an
   has 111 verses. The Báb's commentary contains 111
   Súrihs, which means one Súrih was specifically revealed
   and named by the Báb for each verse of the Qur'an. The
   work contains a total of 9,300 verses.

   The first Súrih, named Súratu'l-Mulk, (Súrih of
   Dominion) was revealed by the Báb for Mullá Husayn

---

37  Bahá'u'lláh , *The Kitáb-i-Iqán*, p. 216.
38  Ibid., p. 231.

Bushrúyih on the night of the 5th of Jamádí, the night of His declaration. Mullá Husayn later presented a number of the verses of this first Súrih to Bahá'u'lláh, which received His praise and acclamation. The balance of the work was revealed gradually over time. According to the beloved Guardian, this blessed and heavenly treatise was translated for the sake of the Persian friends through the exceptional literary genius of Táhirih. The other name of this formidable work is "Qayyúm-ul-Asmá" (Eternal Names), as Yúsuf (Joseph) in the Abjad Numerology is equivalent to the word "Qayyúm" or eternal. Here, by "Qayyúm," the very Person of the Báb is intended. In a letter to His uncle the Báb writes:

> ...and know thou that the number of Yúsuf, (156) is equivalent to "Qayyúm" and the intended reference is to the 'Qá'im of the House of Muhammad' and He is the Living and Self-subsistent. Therefore the first commentary at the dawn of His revelation concerned His own Name....

The expression, 'Ahsanu'l-Qisas' or 'the best story-teller' (and not the best of stories since in the Súrih of Joseph in the Qur'an it is revealed that: "We tell you stories in the best manner") also appears in the Qur'an in the Súrih of Yúsuf.

2. The *Arabic Bayán* was revealed in Máh-Kú. This work is smaller than the Persian Bayán and is also referred to as "Kitábu'l-Jizá" (Book of Chastisement).

3. The *Persian Bayán* was also revealed in Máh-Kú. This work was revealed with specific regard to the number of "Kull-i-Shay" or "all things," the numeric value of which is 361 (the product of 19 x 19). In the Bayán each unity or chapter has 19 "bábs," but only 9 chapters were revealed by the Báb, and the last chapter has only ten bábs. The book comprises a total of some eight thousand verses. The Báb has deferred the revelation of the remainder of the work to the Manifestation of "Baqiyat'u'lláh" or (the Remnant of God). We now know that the Book of Íqán

supplements and completes the Bayán and is revealed to resolve the divine mysteries and secrets found in the sacred books of former religions.

The Bayán includes new commandments and teachings regarding Obligatory Prayer and fasting, marriage and divorce, inheritance, importance of cleanliness, kindness towards animals, prohibition of alcohol and drugs, disapproval of confession before any other human being and ascending of pulpits, etc.—all of which in quite an explicit and definitive manner abrogate the commandments of former religions, include clear reference to the Manifestation of Bahá'u'lláh, and contain counsels on moral issues, explanations on the meaning of concepts such as "Resurrection," "Heaven and Hell," the concept of the "Return," "Standard," "the Hour," and other enigmatic and complex expressions of the Qur'an as well as the Traditions.

4.  *Panj-Sha'n* (Five Modes) is a compilation of Tablets and letters addressed to the spiritual leaders of the Bábí community, where each letter is revealed in five modes or styles: the style of the verse, style of prayer, style of homily, style of commentary, and style of Persian words. This work belongs to the later part of His imprisonment in Chihríq and contains explicit references to the revelation of Bahá'u'lláh as well as His own martyrdom.

5.  The *Commentary on the Súrih of Kawthar*[39] comprises some 2000 verses and was revealed for Vahíd in Shiraz. (In the Qur'an, Súrih of Kawthar is the 108th Súrih, revealed in Mecca and has only three verses.)

6.  The *Commentary on the Súrih of "Val'Asr"*[40] is equivalent to one-third of the Qur'an and was revealed in Isfahan at the request of Muhammad, the Sultánu'l-'Ulamá, King of Divines. (This Súrih, 103rd in the Qur'an, was also revealed in Mecca and also has only three verses. It is the smallest Súrih in the Qur'an.)

---

39  Súrih of Kawthar in the Qur'an was revealed in Mecca and is the smallest Súrih with only three verses.

40  The Súrih of "Val'Asr" was also revealed in Mecca and also contains only three verses

7. The *Commentary on the Al-Há* is another of the important works of the Báb that concerns an account of His afflictions and suffering and the injustices of His opponents and enemies.

8. *Nine Courses of Commentary on the Qur'an* revealed in Máh-Kú were sent to Ibráhím Khalíl. Their whereabouts are unknown.

9. The Báb's famous and significant *address to the Sheriff of Mecca,* a copy of which is extant in which the Sheriff has been addressed by his name, Sulaymán-ibn-i-Owan.

10. The *Letters Addressed to Muhammad Sháh* are three important and well-known works.

11. The *Letters Addressed to Sultán 'Abdu'l-Majíd and Najíb Páshá, governor of Baghdad.*

12. *Letters Addressed to Hájí Mírzá Áqásí,* including the "denunciation homily," which contains strong words of censure and warning. This work was revealed after the Báb's return from Tabriz to Chihríq.

13. *Letters addressed to each of the Iranian religious leaders in various cities and those in Najaf and Karbala.* This includes two letters addressed to Shaykh Muhammad Hasan Isfahani who was a resident of Najaf and the most highly ranked Shiite scholar of his time. In a second letter the Báb tells him,"...We appointed 'Alí and sent him to you. Had you recognized him you would have prostrated yourself before him."

14. *The Seven Qualifications* introduces the seven traits and qualities of the Bábí Faith and is addressed to the early believers of Shiraz. On His return from Mecca, the Báb handed the work to Quddús to take to Shiraz for delivery to Mullá Sádiq Muqaddas. It was after the receipt of this work that Mullá Sádiq chanted the modified version of the "Adhán," which included his bearing witness to the appearance of the new revelation. The events that followed such a bold and flagrant an announcement are detailed in page 13 of this chronicle.

15. *The Seven Proofs,* revealed in Máh-Kú, comprises seven proofs in demonstrating the truth of the revelation of

God, presented in the most graceful and elegant language.

16. *Risálih-i-Ithbát-i-Nabuvvat-i-Khassih (Treatise on Proof of the Exclusivity of Prophethood)* is a proof of the prophethood of the Seal of the Prophets (Muhammad), which was revealed in response to an inquiry by Manúchihr Khán Mu'tamidu'd-Dawlih, the governor of Isfahan, who was a native of the Russian Georgia and a Christian. The work helped him declare his belief in Islam. This treatise was revealed in 50 pages and within a time span of two hours during which Manúchihr Khán himself was present.

17. *Risálih-i-Dhahábiyyih (the Golden Treatise)* was issued in response to a cleric and contains proof of His revelation.

18. *Risálih-i-Sulúk (The Treatise on Spiritual Journey)* which is one of the Báb's early works was possibly revealed even prior to the passing of Siyyid Kázim Rashtí. It brings to light the requirements and conditions of the spiritual journey from self to God. In it, the Báb directly quotes from the writings of the Siyyid and ends the reference by imploring God to lengthen his life, which indicates that the work was revealed in Siyyid's lifetime. The quotation reads:

> ....The main obstacle (on the spiritual journey) is heedlessness and disregard of the divine Providence —Verily this world and the next are but two conditions—if your focus is on God then you are in paradise and if you only look to yourself, then you are in hell. Understand the illusions, break the habits and customs, abandon lust, endure every disloyalty of the people, every reproach of the friend, every rebuke of the enemy and every censure of the spouse and child— then, as you have trodden the path of spiritual attainment you will have opened to your face the gates of God and have fulfilled your desire to enter the Ark of the Generous One....

19. *Risálih–i-Ghiná (the Treatise on Singing)* was revealed in Isfahan and is in response to Sultánu'l-Zákirín, the reciter of the tragedies of Karbala. He had inquired regarding the permissibility of singing of melodies. In response the Báb writes, "From what may be gleaned from the "ahádith" (Traditions) the impermissibility of voice (raised in song) is due to its misdirected effects by those with corrupt inclinations. Otherwise if it does not promote sinfulness and does not overstep the bounds of propriety, then no religious prohibition has been specified." This treatise is quite lengthy.

20. *Risálih-i-Fiqhiyyih (Treatise on Religious Law)* - This treatise, according to Nicolas and as related by Hasan Balyuzi, was revealed by the Báb in His youth when He was engaged as a merchant in Bushihr.

21. *Tablet of Visitation of Sháh 'Abdu'l-'Azím* was revealed on the Báb's sojourn in the village of Kulayn.

22. *Súrih Tawhíd (Súrih of Unity)*

23. *Sahífih A'mál-al-Sunnatih (the Treatise on Acts of Tradition)* was composed of 214 verses in 14 chapters. The Báb declares: "…I swear to Him who is God that if the entire inhabitants of the world were to come together, they would be helpless to generate even a single chapter like it."[41]

24. *Sahifat'ul-'Adliyyih or Risálih-i-'Adliyyih (Treatise on Justice)* is about the beginning and end of all things. This book is different from the "Tablet of Justice" since in Risálih-i-'Adliyyih, the Báb applies the title of "Book of Justice" to the Commentary on the Súrih of Joseph. "Tablet of Justice," a work by Bahá'u'lláh, is addressed to Muhammad Ridá Shahmírzádí who was a Bábí and a survivor of Tabarsi who later discovered the true station of Bahá'u'lláh and became a believer in His Revelation.

25. *Sahífih-i-Baynu'l-Haramayn or Sahífatu'l-Haramayn (Treatise between the two Shrines)* is a response to the questions put to the Báb by Mírzá Muhít Kirmání who considered himself as the most erudite Shaykhí scholar of his time and the worthy successor to Siyyid Kázim

---

41 *Asráru'l-Áthár*, vol. 4, pp. 247-249.

Rashtí. Since it was revealed between Mecca and
Medina, it became known by this title.

26. *Sahífih Ja'fariyyih (Treatise on Ja'far)*
27. *Sahífih Radaviyyih (Treatise on Rida)*
28. *Sahífih Sharh-i-Du'a Ghaybat (Treatise in elucidation
    of the prayer of the Hidden)*
29. *Sahífih Makhzúnih (Treatise of the Hidden)* is one of the
    earliest works of the Báb and comprises various verses
    and prayers.
30. *Furú'-i-'Adliyyih (Branches of Justice)*, according to the
    beloved Guardian, was rendered into Persian by Mullá
    Muhammad Taqí Harátí.
31. *Kitábu'l-Asmá* is divided into 19 units, and each unit
    consists of 19 bábs or chapters that add up to 361
    sections, which is the number of "All Things." Each báb
    is in praise of one of the names of God that is
    manifested by one of the believers.
32. *Kitábu'l-Rúh (the Book of Spirit)* consists of seven
    hundred súrihs and  has been referred to, in the book
    itself by the Báb, as the greatest of Books. This Book was
    revealed during His sojourn in Mecca.
33. *The Tablet of the Hurúfát (Tablet of the Letters)* was
    revealed in Chihríq in honor of Asadu'lláh Khu'í, titled
    Dayyán. Dayyán, having read the Tablet, remarked that
    if the Báb had only revealed this one single Tablet, it
    would have been sufficient evidence of His
    prophethood. Bahá'u'lláh, while in the Most Great
    Prison in Akká revealed a Tablet delineating the many
    illusions and mysteries contained in this work.
34. *Tablet of the Hayákil (Tablet of the Temples)* contains
    19 Temples, each of which has eleven lines, and each
    line numerically adds up to one of God's names.
35. *Various other letters, tablets, treatises and
    commentaries, expositions, prayers, and tablets of
    visitations*, the names of which appear in such works as
    Asráru'l-Áthár (Mystery of the Revealed Works), i.e.,
    the commentary on the Súrih of Baqarih, the account of
    the Day of Áshurá, the Treatise on Resurrection, the
    treatise written in Isfahan for Mírzá Hasan the historian,
    exposition of the Súrih of Qadr, numerous prayers for

the days of the week and the morning prayer,
Ziyáratu'l-Hurúf (Visitation of Letters), Public
Visitation, and separate tablets of visitation for the
Shiite Imams and the high ranking martyrs of the Bábí
revelation, and tens of epistles, expositions,
commentaries, visitation tablets and prayers all of
which are penned by that exalted divine Legislator
Himself or are sealed and signed by Him.

The lofty rank that all of these precious books and treatises
which have issued from the pen of the Báb occupy remains as
yet undisclosed. Perhaps some day scholars with pure hearts
and sanctified souls who are knowledgeable in spiritual verities
and possessed of powerful pens will emerge from behind the
invisible veil of God's Will and will prove able and worthy to
shed light on these miraculous Writings.

Our intention, here, however, was to highlight the
astonishing and unmatched vastness of His Writings in
comparison with scriptures of the past. What is significant is
that all of these works comprise verses revealed through divine
inspiration. There are neither hearsay tales recounted by other
individuals nor personal accounts by anyone of the sayings or
acts of the divine manifestation or any reference to past
historical events.

■ ■ ■

Significantly, the one thing that stands out conspicuously in
the entire range of the Báb's Writings and which through
frequent mention and emphasis is forced to the forefront of His
revelation is His glad-tidings regarding the appearance, in the
person of Bahá'u'lláh, of "Him whom God shall make
manifest." It was already noted before that the Báb's
announcement regarding the appearance of Bahá'u'lláh,
contrary to the allusions made by the entire company of former
prophets, whether major or minor regarding similar events, was
not revealed in implicit or mystical language but rather in clear,
explicit and unequivocal terms. The words of emphasis are so

numerous that it astonishes the mind, since employment of such lucid language for such a pronouncement is unprecedented.

Therefore, rather than continuing with any further definition of the subject, certain verses of the Bayán and other works of the Báb will be presented here so that you may become aware and appreciate the degree of emphasis the Báb employs in order to herald the appearance of the Abhá Beauty:

1. "...the intent of the essence of this chapter is not the Bayán unless it draws attention directly towards 'Him whom God Shall make Manifest'. "

2. "O People of the Bayán: Do not commit what the people of Furqán (the Qur'an) committed and do not hide yourselves from the Beloved for the ascent of the Bayán is towards Him and the joy of His kingdom."

3. "Bayán will not be well pleased with you until you have believed in 'Him whom God shall Make Manifest'."

4. "O People of the Bayán, if you believe in 'Him Whom God Shall Make Manifest', it is you who will profit by acquiring the gift of faith, otherwise He is independent of all things. For example if we place numerous mirrors in front of the sun, its light is reflected in them which tell of its existence, whereas the sun remains free from any association with the mirrors in which it is reflected."

5. "He is like the Sun in the heavens; His verses are His light and the believers are like mirrors in which the Sun appears."

6. "The Manifestation of God in each Dispensation who reflects the eternal Will has been and is the Glory of God before whose glory 'All Things' will be considered as non-existent."

7. And regarding His hidden and open declarations in the years of 9 and 19, He writes: "In the year nine you will come to every blessing."

8. He writes: "In the year nine your thirst for meeting God will be quenched."

9. In a blessed tablet to 'Azím, the Báb writes: "Bide your time until nine years have elapsed from the Bayán, then say 'Blessed is the Lord who is the best of all Creators'."

10. He also saith: "From the start of the revelation until the number of 'unity', be watchful." (In the religion of the Bayán each 'unity' is equivalent to the numeral 19. Nineteen years after the declaration of the Báb, Bahá'u'lláh made his open declaration during Ridván, and in the year 9, He made his secret declaration in the Black Pit in Tihran.)

11. He also saith: "The Lord of the day of Faith will appear at the end of 'unity' and beginning of Thamánín." (Unity in the Abjad numerology is 19, and *Thamánín* in Arabic is 80 and Bahá'u'lláh's declaration took place in 1280 AH (Ridvan of 1863 CE).

12. Also regarding the nearness of the day of revelation of the Promised One and that whenever it takes place, all must obey, He saith: "Be watchful of the time of revelation so that not a moment should separate those who are believers in the Bayán from their acceptance of the new revelation."

13. He also saith: "None knoweth the time of the revelation but God. Whenever it comes, all must submit to the Point of Truth and praise the Lord."

14. He also saith: "If He appears at this moment, I would be the first servant to prostrate (Myself before Him)."

15. Again laying emphasis on the point that belief in the Bayán should not prevent anyone from recognizing God's own manifestation and turn from light to fire, He saith: "No paradise is greater for any soul than the time of God's revelation when he should recognize Him, understand His verses, profess his belief and attain His presence which is the presence of God and soar in the heavenly ocean of His good pleasure."

16. He also saith: "O People of Bayán, do not do what the people of Furqán (Qur'an) did so that you may not nullify the fruits of the faith you garnered while you expected the new revelation."

17. In báb 7 of the second unity of the Persian Bayán, He again saith: "O People of the Bayán, have pity on yourselves and do not nullify the merit of your long wait for the day of resurrection as did the heedless ones of the Qur'an who took pride in Islám for 1270 years

and yet on the day of gathering the fruits of their Faith which was the day of resurrection, the judgment of "unfaithful to Islam" was issued against them...." (The meaning of the day of Resurrection is the day of the appearance of the Tree of Reality, and the duration of the Resurrection is from the onset of the dawning of the new revelation until the setting of Its sun. By the term "Tree of Reality," the person of the Divine Manifestation is intended.

18. And again He saith: "The Bayán and all that is therein should not keep you from that essence of existence and the possessor of the seen and the unseen."

19. And again He saith: If all the believers in the Bayán, declare their belief in 'Him whom God Shall Make Manifest', none will remain in the fire and the judgment of disbelief will not be passed against anyone."

20. In a blessed missive addressed to Mullá Báqir Tabrízí, the Letter of the living, and in response to his question which had also been inquired by the great Vahíd for whom an explanation had been revealed, in a copy of the same response He writes: "You recognized God, then recognize the One that the Lord will manifest who is greater and more exalted than to be perceived by those who are subservient to Him or be identified by testimonies of His creatures and verily I am the first servant to believe in Him and His verses."

21. And in this very missive, He also saith: "If it becomes clear that on the day of His appearance you would not profess your belief in Him, verily I shall seize from you your avowal of faith in this Dispensation since you have not been born except for Him; even if I find that a Christian has professed belief in Him, I would consider him as the apple of my eye and a believer in this revelation without any evidence that might witness to his faith. Thus if that soul in the day of revelation becomes a believer in Him, his worlds will turn into light but if a believer (in Me) remains heedless in that day his worlds will turn into fire."

22. He also saith: "Beware, beware lest in the day of revelation you remain heedless on account of the

Bayán's 'unity' (reference to the Letters of the Living and to the Báb himself), as this 'unity' is but His creation. Beware, beware that you do not remain veiled (from His truth) because of the words of the Bayán as these words are His words in the temple of His former revelation. He is the Sun of Truth and the very face of Oneness, the heavenly countenance, the divine essence and His eternal self."

23. He also adds in this missive: "...Perchance in eight years, in the day of His revelation, you would attain to the presence of God; and thus if you failed to attain His presence at the dawn of revelation, you may attain it at its consummation."

24. And again He saith: "If, on the day of His Revelation, all that are on earth bear Him allegiance, Mine inmost being will rejoice, inasmuch as all will have attained the summit of their existence, and will have been brought face to face with their Beloved, and will have recognized, to the fullest extent attainable in the world of being, the splendor of Him Who is the Desire of their hearts. If not, My soul will indeed be saddened. I truly have nurtured all things for this purpose. How, then, can anyone be veiled from Him? For this have I called upon God, and will continue to call upon Him. He, verily, is nigh, ready to answer."

25. And expressing the degree of His humility and that of His Faith before the threshold of Bahá'u'lláh and the Abhá religion, He saith: "For all that hath been exalted in the Bayán is but as a ring upon My hand, and I Myself am, verily, but a ring upon the hand of Him Whom God shall make manifest—glorified be His mention! He turneth it as He pleaseth, for whatsoever He pleaseth, and through whatsoever He pleaseth. He, verily, is the Help in Peril, the Most High."

26. And again He saith: "O congregation of the Bayán and all who are therein!
 Recognize ye the limits imposed upon you, for such a One as the Point of the Bayán Himself hath believed in Him Whom God shall make manifest, before all things

were created. Therein, verily, do I glory before all who are in the kingdom of heaven and earth."

27. And again He saith: "Today Bayán is in the stage of a seed. The dawn of the appearance of 'He Whom God Shall Make Manifest' is the consummation of the Bayán's duration."

28. In the fifteenth báb of the third unity of the Persian Bayán, He saith: "the Manifestation of God in every revelation that is purposed by the Original Will, has been and is Bahá'u'lláh, before whom 'all things' is considered as nothing….he who declares his belief in 'He Whom God Shall Make Manifest' and His principles has believed in God from the beginning that has no beginning and has emerged under the shadow of His good pleasure and has achieved the merit of His good pleasure in each and all of His revelations. And he who does not profess belief in Him, even though he might have believed and achieved His good pleasure in all His worlds, all would be considered null and void."

29. And again in the sixteenth báb of the second unity He saith: "I swear by 'He Whom God Shall Make Manifest' where no other oath before God is greater, that if He appears and even a single one remains in the Bayán, all punishment will be his lot…."

30. And again He saith: "I counsel the people of the Bayán that if at the time of appearance of 'He Whom God Shall Make Manifest', all achieved the paradise of His nearness and attained His supreme presence then joy be unto you, joy be unto you, joy be unto you…."

31. And again He saith: "…the Bayán, from the beginning to the end, is a testament to all of His attributes and the storehouse of His fire and His light."

32. He also saith: "The whole of the Bayán is but a leaf of the leaves of His paradise."

33. And He also saith: "If you attain to His revelation and remain obedient you would have demonstrated the fruits of the Bayán, otherwise you would not be worthy of mention before God."

34. And again He saith:"No proof for Him or before anyone is greater than His own Being as all the verses and

words emanate from the ocean of His generosity, the sea of His grace and the illuminating rays of His Sun...."

35. And He also saith: "If you but recite one verse of the verses of 'He Whom God Shall Make Manifest', it would be more praiseworthy than transcribing the entirety of the Bayán as that one verse will lead to your salvation whereas the whole of the Bayán will not."

36. And He also saith: "If a soul hears and recites a single verse of His, it would be better than reciting the Bayán a thousand times."

37. And He also saith: "The one year seed of the upcoming revelation is more potent than the whole of what is in the Bayán."

38. And He also saith: "Well is it with him who will witness to the order of Bahá'u'lláh and gives thanks (for the bounty)."

39. And He also saith: "The whole of religion is but His triumph and not the deeds that have been revealed in the Bayán."

40. In Súrih of Joseph He saith: "O Thou Remnant of God! I have sacrificed myself wholly for Thee; I have accepted curses for Thy sake, and have yearned for naught but martyrdom in the path of Thy love. Sufficient witness unto me is God, the Exalted, the Protector, the Ancient of Days."

The Báb's glad tidings regarding the revelation of Bahá'u'lláh are so clear and so numerous that the Pen of the Most High itself bears witness to them: "In no other age or era, has a former religion made mention of the appearance of the subsequent Faith with such clarity and in such detail."

## – Part 3 –

Now let us consider the power and impact of the divinely inspired Words revealed in this heavenly dispensation. Contrary to what we observe in former revelations—where some of the early believers argued with their prophets and others expressed objections and doubts, some while claiming loyalty did not believe His words, and others while professing belief, yet, would not show obedience—in this Faith the effect of the revealed scripture was so extraordinary that the commentary of the Súrih of Joseph so disturbed and overwhelmed Mullá Husayn that when he asked permission to retire from the presence of the Báb, he was told: "If you take your leave now, whoever sees you would say that this youth has gone insane"; the commentary of Súrih of Kawthar so enraptured Vahíd that he had to be revived by rose water sprinkled on his face; a few verses of the commentary of Súrih of Joseph confirmed the great Hujjat and dispatched him and three thousand of his cohorts to the field of martyrdom; a single tablet so enchanted and enthralled the great Dayyán that he traveled the entire distance to Chihríq to visit the Báb on foot; the work, 'the Exclusive Prophethood' so completely transformed and magnetized Manúchihr Khán that he became totally enraptured with the blessed Báb, and Khasá'il-i-Sab'ih (the Seven Qualifications) inspired Mullá Sádiq, such that in the prevailing circumstances of time and place, he publicly and loudly chanted the revised call to prayer which included open reference to the new theophany and as recorded in the non-Bahá'í history books, these wondrous and divinely inspired words sent thousands of the lovers of the blessed Báb, willingly and joyfully to the field of martyrdom the like of which has not been seen in history.

And yet after the martyrdom of the Báb and the declaration of the Abhá Beauty, these same heavenly Writings, each verse of which caused such transformation and attraction, such awe and rapture and which produced such devotees whose unbounded love and self-sacrifice guided them to the field of martyrdom suddenly seemed to lose that miraculous effect as though the Báb, along with His own being had sacrificed the very fruits of

His divine revelation, His revealed words, and their powerful influence in the path of Bahá'u'lláh.

. . .

In elucidation of this point and demonstration of the degree of the influence of the divine verses in this glorious dispensation and so that the conditions and attitudes of the early believers at the time of the appearance of the Báb are more fully appreciated, a brief comparative evaluation is undertaken below.

As per the text of the Old Testament, in the Book of Exodus when Moses returned from Mount Sinai to His people, the Israelites, He discovered that His followers had fashioned a golden calf that had become the subject of their worship. And thus, aided by the members of the House of Levi to which He belonged, Moses, in one day, killed three thousand of the believers.

"And all the Levites rallied to him. He said to them, 'Thus says the Lord, the God of Israel: Each of you put sword on thigh, go back and forth from gate to gate throughout the camp, and slay brother, neighbor, and kin.' The Levites did as Moses had bidden and some three thousand of the people fell that day." (Exodus 32: 27–29). This is a sample of the spiritual maturity and devotion of the people who believed in Moses at the time of appearance.

Jesus Christ, at the time of His martyrdom had some 150 believers of whom 12 were the disciples, Peter, Andrew, Simon, James, Judas, Philip, Bartholomew, Matthew, John, and Thomas. It was Judas who, despite Jesus' knowledge of his intent, revealed His hiding place for a few pieces of silver leading to His arrest and crucifixion. The rest of the disciples at the time of Jesus' arrest and trial fled the area, and Peter who was the first to believe in Him and whom Jesus had chosen as the foundation upon which to build His church, on the night of the crucifixion, denied Him three times and even took an oath that he did not know Him and went so far as cursing His name. And it was not until the second "crowing of the cock" that he remembered

Jesus' remark that until that second "crowing of the cock" you will have denied me three times. He then went out and wept.[42]

This too is an example of the faith and devotion of the early Christian believers at the time of Jesus.

Regarding the believers in Muhammad and the unseemly conduct of some of them against the prophet, though supported by the Qur'an and the credible traditions of both Sunni and Shia, I will withhold comments since if misunderstood it could result in the martyrdom of a few other innocent friends or the imprisonment of a group of blameless and obedient believers. Otherwise reference, supported by historical evidence, may easily be made of assorted cases of disobedience of a number of the believers to the instructions of the Messenger of God, a few of which are as follows:

1. Disobedience of the believers in the battle of Ohud.
2. Weakness in belief of some of the followers in the promises of God's Messenger regarding their ultimate victory over Khusraw (the Persian Emperor) and Caesar. They claimed that: "Mohammad has promised us the treasurers of Khusraw and Caesar and yet we can't even relieve our bodily functions in peace."[43]
3. Disobedience of some of the followers, one of whom later became the second Caliph of Islam, to Muhammad's instructions in His deathbed. In response to Messenger of God's request to be given pen and paper so that He may write His testament, some of those present said: "Pain has overcome the prophet. The Qur'an is before us and God's words are sufficient unto us." It is said that Omar made this comment.

There was immediate disagreement among the rank of the believers. Some insisted that Muhammad should be given the chance to write down such instructions that would prevent the believers from being misguided in the future. Others did not see the necessity for this and considered the Book of God as complete and final. Witnessing the argument, Muhammad

---

42 Matthew 26:74-75.
43 M. H. Haykal, *Life of Muhammad*, translated by A. Payandeh, p. 458.

asked them to leave and added that it was not seemly to quarrel in the presence of the Prophet of God.

After this event Ibn-i-'Abbás felt that the Muslims, by denying the Prophet the opportunity to write His last thoughts, destroyed something very important, but Omar remained adamant and contended that the verse in the Qur'an which says: "We have verily not fallen short in revealing the Word is adequate proof of the completeness of divine instructions."[44]

. . .

But in the blessed revelation of the Primal Point (the Báb), thousand of believers, with unbounded courage and in the path of His love, sacrificed their lives in the field of martyrdom, stories of whose heroic deeds are recorded in non-Bahá'í accounts as well.

1.  Watson, the author of the *History of the Qájár* writes: "The Bábís confronted their destiny with fearless power none of whom could be forced to recant their faith and accept Islam as their religion so that they may escape the gallows. As the burning candle burned into the flesh of one of Báb's followers, one of the judges tried to convince him to curse the name of the Báb so that he may live. He in turn cursed the judge's name…. He was in such high spirits that torture and agony seemed to have little effect on him."[45]

2.  Gustov Lebon, the renowned French physician, psychologist, sociologist, philosopher, and author (1841–1931), in his book *Beliefs and Ideas* writes: "In Tabriz a famous Bábí was arrested and was taken to the town's square. Whatever they did so that he should curse his Faith in order to escape death, he refused. Acting as intermediaries, town merchants asked him to utter only one word in renunciation of his beliefs; he would not accept. They threatened him with the life of his child. He laid himself on the ground and told them

---

44  Ibid.
45  Quoted in M. Moshrefzadeh, *The Bahá'í Faith Has a Divine Origin.*

to kill the child on his breast. They brought his child. His older child who was 14 ran forward and told them that he was older and that he should be the first to give his life....Then they martyred both sons of the Bábí.

He also writes that they suspended, upside down, a Bábí from the top of the city wall and as he approached death he was heard whispering: "O, my beloved, have I gained Thy good pleasure?"

In *God Passes By*, the beloved Guardian quotes a number of remarks and testimonies of some Western writers:

3.  "Renan writes: thousands came to the field of sacrifice, with boundless joy and excitement in the path of the Báb."

4.  Browne writes: "A shining example of the power of faith, devotion, will to sacrifice and pure courage has manifested itself in the dawning of the Bábí religion. The spirit of devotion and faith, detachment and spiritual awareness which animates the Bábís is so powerful and inspiring that can magnetize anyone who comes into contact with it, a Faith that one day may rank as the most distinguished among the company of the great religions of the world." (*God Passes By*, page 80)

5.  Professor J. Darmushteter writes: "The Bábí Faith that within less than five years spread from one end of Iran to the other and in the year 1852 witnessed the bloodshed of so many of its adherents, now in utmost dignity and self-assurance is progressing and gaining a loftier and more exalted status."[46]

6.  Lord Curzon writes: "In the blood-stained pages of Bábí history there are numerous astonishing tales of devotion and sacrifice of this people that is a tribute to the greatness of that Faith.... It is but obvious that religious teachings that can generate such spirit of detachment and ready sacrifice of life in its followers and create in them such level of steadfastness and high mindedness

---

46  Shoghi Effendi, *God Passes By*.

must be considered most noble and commendable."
(Quoted in *God Passes By*, page 80)

7.  Count de Gobineau writes: "I must admit that if I had
    found in Europe a group of people similar to the Bábís
    evincing that same degree of devotion, passion and
    power of attraction as well as steadfastness, purity of
    heart and love for the entire humankind, I would have
    surely accepted their beliefs. Their power to create fear
    in the hearts of their enemies and yet their intense love
    and ardent penchant in teaching and guiding seekers as
    well as their unexpected success in attracting people of
    every class and rank convinced me that in a short time
    the control of governance will fall into their hands and
    the scepter of power and authority would ultimately
    rest in their grasp."[47]

8.  Watson, author of the *History of Qájár* writes: "In
    comparison, it may be concluded that the followers of
    the Báb were more faithful than those of Muhammad. In
    the early years after its advent this Faith spread much
    faster than Christianity."

9.  Sir Francis Edward Younghusband (1863–1942) writes
    as follows about the Báb: "… Moved by the penetrating
    power of His words, thousands of the poor and the
    well-to-do, scholar and illiterate, young and old,
    sacrificed their lives, accepted all manner of
    persecution, agony and torture and bore all of this with
    steadfastness, quiescence and submission."[48]

10. 'Abbás Qulí Khán Láríjání, one of the commanders of
    the Tabarsi struggle whose bullet felled the martyred
    Mullá Husayn, related, some two years after the
    incident, stories regarding the conflict in a gathering
    and in the presence of Prince Ahmad Mírzá as related in
    the book Zuhúru'l-Haqq (Revelation of Truth). He
    remembered: "O great Prince, what can I say and how
    can I describe the conduct of those Bábís? It is truly a
    story that is incredible and astonishing. Those who have
    heard the stories of the tragedy of Karbala and the

47  Quoted in Shoghi Effendi, *God Passes By*.
48  Quoted in *Some Bahá'í Discussions*.

martyrdom of Imam Husayn[49] and wished they could
witness with their own eyes those heart-rending scenes
and the demeanor and bearing of that wronged one of
the world before his cruel oppressors, should have been
in Tabarsi so that they could witness the exact same
scenes. The conditions and the intensity of the events
were such that one even forgot those similar historical
events, as Mullá Husayn and his companions, in the
same manner as the Prince of Martyrs and his followers,
presented themselves in the field of sacrifice and my
troops and I, with drawn swords and rifles made ready
to meet them. For Mullá Husayn and his companions
killing and dying seemed the same. I don't know what
these Bábís have seen and experienced that they
competed with each other with joy and delight to meet
their deaths. They exhibited no fear and met the guns
head on and seemed to consider the sharp blade and the
blood shedding dagger as their ultimate salvation and
the key to eternal life. Even though starving and
without any source of food and water and lacking in
rest and recuperation which had made them feeble and
vulnerable, yet at the hour of battle they seemed to have
been infused with fresh power and renewed spirit and
therefore they gained such boldness and courage that
the minds of the wise are incapable of understanding."

These and hundreds of similar events as testified by non-
Bahá'í sources bear witness to the greatness of the faith and
devotion of the Bábís and only a few were quoted here since

> *Lovers' secrets are better revealed*
> *By others' chronicles of events and deeds*

Otherwise, you beloved of God are all well aware of the
epic events of Tabarsi, Zanján, Niyríz, Yazd, Tihran and
Khurásán, Isfahan, and other cities of Iran. Praised be God, how
numerous the number of the lovers who danced to the field of
sacrifice and offered sweet pastry among the onlookers, how
many of them asked the executioner to let them be first, and

---

49  Imam Husayn was martyred in Karbala.

how many who tried to ease the executioner's conscience of his misgivings in committing such horrible acts, how many who kissed the executioner's hand and chanted songs of love, all of whom as attested by Bahá'u'lláh gave their lives and yet did not utter a single unseemly word. Their most sublime example was Anís who in the field of sacrifice placed his head upon the breast of His incomparable Beloved so that his head may receive the volley of the bullets.

The best Beloved, the Primal Point and the exalted Lord, the Báb who had sent thousands of God intoxicated lovers of His beauty to the field of martyrdom, Himself led the field and placed His breast before hundreds of bullets, and thus sacrificed His blessed Self as well as the majestic power and influence of the religion of Bayán, its most renowned and distinguished believers, its elder cast, and His most eminent companions and devotees, utterly and unreservedly, all in the path of the Remnant of God, the Abhá Beauty, the Promised One of all Faiths, the Desired One of all humankind, the Beloved of hearts and Subject of love and devotion of all who are endowed with the gift of faith, Bahá'u'lláh.

So all-embracing was this act of sacrifice that after the revelation of Bahá'u'lláh and except for certain laws such as sanctioning interest on money, limiting the size of dowry, instituting the Right of God, the waiting period prior to divorce, kindness to animals, proscription in carrying firearms, prohibition of confessing of sin to any individual, banning of ascending pulpits, prohibition of congregational prayer except for the prayer for the dead, and others which now as part of the Aqdas form the laws of the Bahá'í Faith, a religion known as the Bábí Faith, ceased to exist. None remained from His devoted followers and self-sacrificing believers, and no trace of the supernatural influence of its divine teachings endured; all of which vanished or reappeared in the supreme religion of Bahá'u'lláh, except for its matchless history and grandeur, and tale of its imperishable and heroic episodes which became timeless and shone better and brighter than any other historical spectacle; it was inscribed in the memory of the friends and stored safe in the heart of its lovers and recorded in the works of writers and documented in the books of historians.

The world of love found a new song and the lovers'
minstrel discovered a new melody. Sacrifice became the secret
of true life and evanescence lead to glory; the world of dust
became illumined and the God's kingdoms shone brightly by
the heavenly light of so many pure souls....

This tale is unfinished. It is a story of love, eternal and
everlasting....what was recounted was merely a passing glance.

> *In clamor are the seven domes of the firmament with*
> *this saga*
>
> *Consider the shortsighted who sufficed with but a*
> *brief tale.*

## Selected Sources

-----. *Má'idih-i-Ásmání* (9 volumes from the Writings of Bahá'u'lláh, 'Abdu'l-Bahá and the Guardian). Compiled by Mr. Ishráq Khávari.

-----. *The Bible* (Old and New Testaments).

-----. *The Qur'an.*

'Abdu'l-Bahá. *Makátíb* (8 volumes).

'Abdu'l-Bahá. *Maqáliyyih Shakhsí Sayyáh* (*A Traveler's Narrative*).

Báb, The. *Bayán.*

Bahá'u'lláh. *Kitáb-i-Iqán* (*The Book of Certitude*).

Balyuzi, H. M. *Bahá'u'lláh.*

Balyuzi, H. M. *The Báb.*

Faizi, Muhammad 'Alí. *Afnán Dynasty.*

Faizi, Muhammad 'Alí. *La'álí-i-Dirakhshán* (*The Brilliant Gems*).

Furutan, 'Alí Akbar. *A Few Discussions on the Cause.*

Ghadimi, Riaz. *Christianity and Its Branches.*

Ghadimi, Riaz. *Siyyid'ur-Rusul, His Holiness Muhammad, Islam and its branches.*

Khávarí, Ishráq. *Asrár-i-Rabbání.*

Khávarí, Ishráq. *Calendar of the History of the Cause.*

Khávarí, Ishráq. *Ganj-i-Sháyigán* (*The Precious Treasure*).

Khávarí, Ishráq. *Qámús-i-Iqán* (4 volumes).

Khávarí, Ishráq. *Rahíq-i-Makhtúm* (*The Choice Sealed Wine*, 2 volumes).

Khávarí, Ishráq. *Risálih-i-Ayyam-i-Tis'ih.*

Lobon, Gustav. *Árá va 'Aqáyid.*

Mázandarání, Fádil. *Asrár-ul-Áthár.*

Mázandarání, Fádil. *Rahbarán va Rahruván* (*Leaders and Followers*).

Mázandarání, Fádil. *Zuhúru'l-Haqq* (*Revelation of Truth,* 3 volumes).

Momen, Mooján. *The Bábí and Bahá'í Religions (1844-1944).*

Moshrefzadeh, M. *The Bahá'í Faith has a Divine Source.*

Samandar, Shaykh Kázim. *History of Samandar.*

Shoghi Effendi. God Passes By (*Book of Qarn-i-Badi'*, 4 volumes). Farsi translation by Nasrulláh Maviddat.

Zarandí, Nabíl. *The Dawn-Breakers: Nabíl's Narrative of the Early Days of the Bahá'í Revelation.*

## Other Educational Publications by the Same Author

1. The book "Jamál-i-Abhá, Hadrat-i-Bahá'u'lláh, Jalla Ismih'ul'A'lá" (The Abhá Beauty, Bahá'u'lláh) (2$^{nd}$ Printing, Canada)
2. Gulzár-i-Ta'lím- Bahá'í (The Rose Garden of Bahá'í Teachings), containing 105 reproductions of authoritative texts related to 120 subject matters, Published in Germany
3. "Some Bahá'í Authoritative Texts Regarding Personal Virtues and Rules Regarding Consultation", Second Printing, Canada
4. "A Pamphlet on the History of Religions", 2$^{nd}$ Printing, Canada
5. "Two Thousand Words", Repeated Printing in Iran
6. "Six Thousand Words" with contribution by Mr. Ihsánulláh Hemmat, Second Printing, Germany
7. "Dictionary of Selected Words" or "Nineteen Thousand Words", 2$^{nd}$ Printing, Canada
8. The Book "The Lord of Prophets, Muhammad, Islám and its Branches", Canada
9. The Book "Hadrat-i-Rúh, Jesus, Son of Mary, Christianity and its Branches", Canada

www.ingramcontent.com/pod-product-compliance
Lightning Source LLC
Chambersburg PA
CBHW020518030426
42337CB00011B/445